Jeremy V. Jones

Walking
on Water

Regal

From Gospel Light
Ventura, California, U.S.A.

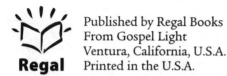

Published by Regal Books
From Gospel Light
Ventura, California, U.S.A.
Printed in the U.S.A.

Regal Books is a ministry of Gospel Light, a Christian publisher dedicated to serving the local church. We believe God's vision for Gospel Light is to provide church leaders with biblical, user-friendly materials that will help them evangelize, disciple and minister to children, youth and families. It is our prayer that this Regal book will help you discover biblical truth for your own life and help you meet the needs of others. May God richly bless you.

For a free catalog of resources from Regal Books/Gospel Light, please call your Christian supplier or contact us at 1-800-4-GOSPEL *or* www.regalbooks.com.

All Scripture quotations are taken from the *Holy Bible, New International Version®*. Copyright © 1973, 1978, 1984 by International Bible Society. Used by permission of Zondervan Publishing House. All rights reserved.

Special thanks to Walking on Water Ministries for use of selected quotes from the following videos: *Changes,* Edward Feuer and Bryan Jennings, Walking on Water Foundation, 2000; *The Outsiders,* Jesse Schluntz and Bryan Jennings, Walking on Water Foundation, 2002; and *Noah's Arc,* Nic McLean and Bryan Jennings, Walking on Water Foundation, 2004.

Photographs reprinted courtesy of DJ Struntz, Noah Hamilton, AJ Neste, ASP World Tour and Walking on Water Ministries.

Library of Congress Cataloging-in-Publication Data
Jones, Jeremy.
  Walking on water / Jeremy Jones.
    p. cm.
  Includes bibliographical references.
  ISBN 0-8307-4285-9 (trade paper)
  1. Surfers—Religious life. 2. Surfing—Religious aspects—Christianity. I. Title.
BV4596.S93J66 2006
248.8'8—dc22   2006017481

1   2   3   4   5   6   7   8   9   10   /   10   09   08   07   06

Rights for publishing this book in other languages are contracted by Gospel Light Worldwide, the international nonprofit ministry of Gospel Light. Gospel Light Worldwide also provides publishing and technical assistance to international publishers dedicated to producing Sunday School and Vacation Bible School curricula and books in the languages of the world. For additional information, visit www.gospellightworldwide.org; write to Gospel Light Worldwide, P.O. Box 3875, Ventura, CA 93006; or send an e-mail to info@gospellightworldwide.org.

FOR ASPEN

May you know the joys of walking on water and living in the flow of your Creator.

Contents

Acknowledgments

Many thanks to . . .

My wife, Janna, for her patient support, invaluable assistance and unconditional love, especially while I wrote this book.

All the surfers who shared their time, thoughts and personal stories to bring life to this book.

Bryan Jennings, for his encouragement, insight and surf lessons long ago.

Michael Ross, for his patience, encouragement and good advice.

My brother-in-law Saul Levine, for letting me borrow his boards and wetsuits, taking me surfing, and fueling the stoke.

Roger Thompson, Alex Field and the Regal team for catching the vision and bringing the concepts into this final product. Mark Weising, Rose Decaen and Jennifer Cullis for lending your editorial eyes. Marlene Baer, Jessica Jones and Michelle Basich for helping to get the word out. Rob Williams and Josh Talbot for their creativity and design.

The guy at the Hanalei Board Swap for selling me my first board: an 8-foot, 6-inch Brewer.

The independent coffee merchants of Colorado Springs—Candlelight Coffee Lounge, Boulder Street Roasters, Pikes Perk, Rico's, It's a Grind—for providing me with an office away from the office and caffeine to fuel the creative process.

God, for revealing intricate love in His vast creation.

Foreword

The sport of surfing has always fascinated people and rightly so. It is a unique sport where the athlete and nature must work together in an attempt to capture the perfect moment. Being so closely connected to God's creation, it is no wonder why most surfers are spiritually minded people. Whether riding a 50-foot wave or a 1-foot wave, surfing is definitely a spiritual experience. When I caught my first wave, something happened inside my 10-year-old heart.

Twenty-two years, many strong friendships, thousands of waves ridden, a professional surfing career, a surf camp established, four surf documentaries, and a growing love and respect of God and His ocean have occurred since that first ride in La Jolla, California, in 1984. And since 1995, Walking on Water Foundation's purpose has been to impact this generation with the love of Jesus Christ through the sport of surfing by means of our surf camps and documentaries.

Jeremy Jones has been a good friend and support to Walking on Water for the past eight years. He has spent time at the Walking on Water surf camps, and I have been blessed personally by his love for people and specifically for youth. God works in mysterious ways. He chose some fishermen and a tax collector to be His disciples. In the '70s, He used hippies in the Jesus Movement. I believe He wants a people group who are willing to go when and where He desires. Surfers make perfect messengers because they are used to traveling the world in search of the perfect wave, eating whatever is available, and sleeping wherever they can. Surfers are flexible people willing to take risks.

Enjoy the stories of those in these pages who are doing just that to follow God's leading and to walk on water.

Bryan Jennings, Founder, Walking on Water Foundation

The Spirit of Surfing

Surfing is a spiritual experience.

If you've ever paddled out, waited for a set or even a shore-breaking ripple to roll in, and then dropped in on your first wave, you understand the joy. When you're surfing, you're interacting with nature in one of its most dynamic and vast forms. There's no other feeling like it. Experiencing that adrenaline rush keeps you coming back for more and more—maybe even to the point of religious fervor.

Surfers have long been looked down on (or admired, depending on your perspective) for their willingness to drop everything else when their favorite breaks are firing. They sing with rapturous language the praises of their sessions in the sea. In fact, in his interesting and entertaining 2005 article, "Is God a Goofyfoot?" author Brad Melekian wondered whether surfing could actually meet the criteria to be classified as a world religion and even tested his theory.[1]

Ask most wave riders and they'll describe some deep connection with the water, the waves or the power of the sea. Yet it's a sense of connection with something far beyond ourselves. The vast scope of the ocean is humbling. It covers nearly three-fourths of our planet and holds secrets that we humans have yet to discover. To be swept into the rhythms of the deep is to be drawn into a greater awareness of the infinite cosmic forces surrounding us.

The ancient Hawaiians, the inventors of this beautiful sport, offered prayers and gifts to the gods, hoping for good waves. Many surfers still turn their worshipful adoration to the sea itself or the mystical forces they associate with it.

But then there are those who follow the guidance of the liquid creation to an even mightier Creator. They realize that as fulfilling as surfing can be, it will leave us ultimately unfulfilled, and that as transcendent as it can seem, it will leave us empty again on the shore. They have experienced an indescribable love and peace and have discovered an unfathomable gratitude for what they know they don't deserve: a living, breathing relationship with the One who made the winds and the waves and the vast depths of all we are surrounded by.

I hope this book will give you a glimpse into these realms. The idea for this book was born out of the fulfillment of a dream with lifelong roots: a sabbatical in Hawaii with my young family, surfing every day. And its pages grew out of inspiration by real surfers living real spiritual lives.

I had wanted to ride waves since my teens when I had plastered my bedroom walls with photo spreads from surf magazines, but living far from the ocean had always been an obstacle. I had managed to catch a few waves here and there, but the extended time in Hawaii allowed me to discover fully the joys of wave-sliding.

Friendships and growing connections with other surfers revealed that a growing number of surfers have a passion for God that outranks even their passion for the waves. These individuals exist across the spectrum of the surf culture. They are grommets and top-ranking pros, ministry heads and industry executives, company reps and team riders, influential shapers and photographers and artists. They are men and women, boys and girls, husbands and wives, parents and children. And they are all bound together by a shared love for the ocean and a shared love for Jesus.

God is at work in surfing. Sure, God is at work in the entire world of which surfing is a microcosm. But He is moving in the lives of surfers, uniting them, and using them to accomplish His goals like never before. It's ironic that the first missionaries to intersect with surfing essentially brought the sport to an end for decades, nearly killing it off completely. Now the missionaries are surfers using the activity and lifestyle to bring divine love to others at their local breaks and around the world.

And who better to do so? For the most part, surfers are laid-back and flexible, yet passionate and ready when conditions are right. They share a deep bond with fellow wave riders. Surfers know how to keep it real.

In this book are the stories of top wave riders and watermen who share a similar spiritual awareness. They are surfers at their core and followers of Jesus, living out a personal faith on a public platform. They are not theologians. They are not perfect. They simply share an understanding that the Creator of the waves and the powers of the deep also created them and that He desires to know and relate with them.

Follow their spiritual journeys as they attempt to walk with God in an authentic way. Follow the finger of God moving across the waters of the surfing culture. Follow the stoke to the waves and beyond.

C.J. Hobgood: World Champion

So it was down to this, the final contest of the year: the Rip Curl Cup at Sunset Beach, Hawaii. C.J. Hobgood had started the day narrowly leading the points race, but eight hungry competitors now trailed close enough to be within range of surpassing him and claiming the title for themselves. A victory at this event would secure the world championship for the 22-year-old Floridian.

If only it was that easy.

The day's second-round heats began well for C.J. as friend and fellow-Floridian Ben Bourgeois knocked veteran Mark Occilupo out of contention. Brazilian Renan Rocha also contributed to C.J.'s cause by defeating rising star Andy Irons.

It looked as if C.J. might continue to control his own destiny, as he carried a narrow points margin over wildcard and Rip Curl trials winner Myles Padaca. But with the final seconds ticking away in their heat, Padaca converted one final wave into enough points to overtake C.J.'s narrow 2.32-point edge. C.J. was sent to the shore.

His chances didn't look good: The six remaining competitors needed only to advance to the semifinals to overtake the points lead and lay claim to the championship. C.J. stayed off the beach for the rest of the contest, expecting the worst but hoping for the best.

Vitals

Born: July 6, 1979

Home: Satellite Beach, Florida

Family: wife, Rachel, and daughter, Genevieve

Sponsors: Globe, Body Glove, Bill Johnson Shapes, Smith, X-Trak, Fin Control System (FCS), Vestal

Big Moment: 2001 ASP World Championship

More: www.hobgoods.com

But the surprise eliminations continued. First, Sunny Garcia went down to the hard-charging Mick Fanning, and the then-No. 3 Cory Lopez lost to Shane Beschen. The next contender to disappear was No. 4 Taylor Knox, followed by No. 7 Shane Powell of Australia. Only Jake Patterson and the ninth-ranked Australian Danny Wills remained.

Hawaiian Kalani Robb came through on C.J.'s behalf in the final minutes of his second-round heat by taking out Powell. That left Bourgeois in position to do his friend a second favor of the day. And what a favor it was: Bourgeois dominated the heat and sent Wills paddling out in defeat.

"You couldn't write as good a story if you were thinking the most fiction stuff," C.J. would later tell *Surfing* magazine.[1] The contest continued, but ultimately C.J. claimed the 2001 world title. It was only his third year on the Association of Surfing Professionals (ASP) World Championship Tour.

Although C.J. realized his great debt to Bourgeois, he offered his public thanks first to Jesus. "[Jesus] pretty much is my life, and I try to be on his path," he says. "He has given me everything that I have; this has nothing to do with me at all. I'm stoked to be able to thank Jesus Christ for everything. I'm able to enjoy all I have so much more because of that."[2]

For C.J., it was a meteoric rise to the pinnacle of pro surfing. Yet it was this very quest to fulfill his lifelong dreams that initially revealed a spiritual emptiness within. As C.J. strove to achieve surfing's highest awards, his path eventually led him to surrender his life to the God who controls the wind and the waves.

EAST COAST KID

Like many other surfers, C.J.'s first wave-riding experiences took place back in his preschool days. Thanks to his lifelong surfing dad, Clifton, C.J. and his brother, Damien, were boogie boarding at age 4 and stand-up riding at 6. Clifton passed on his passion to his oldest son well. He passed on his name, too: "C.J." stands for "Clifton James."

"Our parents loved the beach, and that was a way that we could all get out of the house," C.J. says. It also didn't hurt that the twins had only a five-minute bike ride to the break at Satellite Beach, which provided them with plenty of time for practice. Every afternoon was similar: race home from school, throw down the book bags, grab the boards, and bolt for the beach.

"Back then, all I could ever think about was how fast I could get home and go surfing," C.J. told *Transworld Surf.* "When contest weekends came around, I'd be thinking about the contest. Or if there wasn't a contest, I'd be thinking about getting a new board, or watching surf videos and deciding which pro I was going to imitate for my friends during our next freesurf."[3]

Both Hobgoods were involved in team sports, including soccer and baseball. "I was the pitcher, and Damien was the catcher,"

C.J. says. But surfing conquered all after the bros got their first taste of contest surfing when they were 10. Both came home with a trophy, and from that time on they were hooked. No more playing all season for a chance to bag some team hardware. With the mad skills the 'Goods had, every competition provided a realistic shot at instant victory gratification.

It wasn't long before the boys were attracting a lot of attention and receiving sponsorships. At 13 they went national, appearing in a *Sports Illustrated for Kids* photo spread. One two-page shot captured the essence of Hobgood childhood: It depicted the brothers on their bikes at the beach with their boards in hand.

C.J. and Damien continued to hone their skills at Sebastien Inlet, the East Coast's premier wave, where they had the opportunity to observe and learn from Kelly Slater and former pro stars Matt Kechele, Charlie Kuhn and Bill Hartley. At 16, both made the U.S. Surf Team and continued their assault on the National Scholastic Surfing Association (NSSA). By the time he was 17, C.J. had claimed five regional and national NSSA championships.

Despite the success, C.J. kept a humble and grounded outlook. He maintains that he was never billed as the next Slater and that it was his hard work that brought him so far.

NEXT STEP

"I'm not very patient," C.J. says.

But he is a fearless, hard-charging competitor both in and out of the water. Perhaps the combination of these traits fueled his rapid ascent to the top of the ASP.

"When I was 18, I thought, I can do this and *I can make it. I can make a living, be productive, you know. I'm gonna surf the rest of my life*

*whether it is competitive or not, but, yeah, I can do it [make it profession-
ally],"* C.J. says.

In 1998, C.J. screamed through the World Qualifying Series,
qualifying for the top-flight World Championship Tour in only one
year. It usually takes even exceptionally talented surfers three to five
years to move up. Not to be one struggling at the lower ranks of the
world's then top 44, C.J. claimed the 1999 Rookie of the Year award
and entered the elite ranks at No. 18. In 2000, he brought home the
hardware as the Most Improved Surfer, jumping 11 spots to finish
the year ranked No. 7. And, as you already know, the 2001 season
closed with C.J. claiming the World Champion title.

UNSATISFIED

In the eyes of many a grom and adult surfer alike, C.J. had it all.
But behind all the public success, a sense of deep personal unrest
was growing within C.J. He was realizing his potential and achieving his dreams of reaching the pro ranks of surfing, but doing so
had left him with a feeling of emptiness rather than the satisfac-
tion he had expected. "I realized that no matter what I did in this
world, no matter what I tried to accomplish or tried to achieve or
get, it wasn't happiness," C.J. says.

Like his brother, Damien, C.J. had been raised in the Catholic
church. Their mother taught Sunday School, and C.J. had learned
a lot about God. But, admittedly, he had no relationship with God.
"It was like God was an hour on Sunday, but I still had my life," C.J.
said in the Walking on Water film *Noah's Arc.*

As C.J. continued his rise through the surf world, he began to
hear about changes that were taking place within a crew of surfers
on North Carolina's Outer Banks. C.J. went back to grommethood

with some of those surfers, such as Noah Snyder and Jesse Hines. From their teens, the two East Coast crews had regularly road-tripped back and forth to make the most of hurricane-season Hatteras and warm-water Florida.

Word was that Noah and the whole crew had accepted Jesus. C.J. heard the news, but he didn't dwell on it. However, over the course of the next few years, C.J. began to notice that these guys were different. Instead of partying, they were conducting Bible studies. Although they had always been friendly, they now began to demonstrate a genuine concern for their friends. C.J. could see that something had changed. The Hatteras crew was living out God's love.

Buddy Favor was C.J.'s longtime roommate. While driving back to Florida from North Carolina, Buddy heard how God had changed Noah's life and decided to surrender his life to Christ. Buddy was now a new man, too, and the spiritual growth he experienced began to rub off on C.J.

"The snowball started going on up [in the Outer Banks], and we had our own little snowball that started going on down our way," C.J. says in *Noah's Arc*. "How thankful I am that Noah shared with Buddy and that ultimately his faith started affecting my life. Going back and putting fingerprints on everything, I'm thankful that God was working in people's lives and ultimately in my life."

In the summer of 2000, C.J. placed control of his life in Christ's hands at Calvary Chapel in Melbourne, Florida. "I think a lot of people find the Lord when they are either at their lowest point or their highest point," C.J. says. "I think I came to the Lord at the highest time, because I realized that no matter what I did in this world, no matter what I tried to accomplish or tried to achieve or tried to get, it was not happiness. I was reaching my dream to make the world tour, and right when I reached that dream is when God was right there in my face."

C.J. maintains that even though he had a choice about accepting or rejecting Christ, God's call was too powerful to resist: "I think there is a time when the Lord calls you, and no matter what, if He wants you, He is going to get you."

LIFE IN THE SPOTLIGHT

The process of encountering and eventually surrendering one's life to Christ is highly personal and often unique. Although it perhaps represents life's deepest transformation, becoming a new creation, as the Bible describes it, can provide some interesting challenges when it occurs in the public spotlight.

This is especially true in the world of professional sports, and surfing is no exception. Camaraderie can quickly become overshadowed by a serious competitive streak. Image means everything to the potential corporate sponsors who finance the travel expenses necessary for a surfer to keep up with a worldwide roster of events—thus making or breaking that surfer's ability to pay the bills.

In the beginning of his new spiritual life, C.J. was well aware of the scene and had some fears about how his newfound faith might be perceived. He remembers thinking at the time, *Nobody's going to like me on tour. There are all these people I look up to who are not going to want to hang out or talk to me because I'm, like, a weirdo and blah, blah, blah.*

But what initially felt awkward became more natural as C.J.'s new faith began to deepen and he realized that God had placed him in the spotlight for a purpose.

"It was like Damien and I needed to take the smallest step of faith, and God would use it for His glory so much," C.J. says. "That's always been His thing. I was talking to God, saying, *I do this little step, and You take it and blow it up. There are missionaries and people who do a lot of things all about God. I do what I love. I surf. I say a few things, and You are taking it and using it for Your glory. You're making me think I'm some, like, preacher guy who knows everything about You. What's going on here? Let me get my act together a little bit more before You start going crazy."*

When you've found the peace and fulfillment that have long eluded you, it's natural to talk about it even if you do have some initial concerns about how you'll be perceived. C.J. and Damien were presented quickly with plenty of opportunities to represent their faith on the public stage. Both appeared in the Christian films *The Outsiders* and *Noah's Arc.* They continue to be questioned regularly about their spiritual lives by both secular and Christian journalists. And they receive invitations to speak to churches and other Christian groups.

Perhaps it's the 'Goods' willingness to be real with others— fellow pros, industry representatives, friends, media and fans— that has helped them maintain their high level of respect in the surf community. (Their rad surfing talents help too, of course.) The guys are genuine and humble.

"The thing I respect most about C.J. and Damien is humility," film producer Matt Katsolis says. "A five-second walk off the beach takes them a half hour because they make eye contact with each kid, shake hands, truly listen to him and take the time to encourage him by telling him things like, 'Oh, you're surfing? That board's too big for you. Try this.' That blows my mind. It's not a front they put on for any video; they are like that. They are respected and well known—both are in the Top 10 in the world—yet they treat every person with so much respect and dignity."

C.J. is also honest, even about his own shortcomings. When questioned for a 2003 *Transworld Surf* article about living as a Christian on the World Championship Tour, C.J. spoke honestly about his failures within the ASP's world-class party scene and about his struggles to maintain sexual purity after a not-so-spotless past. (He was not yet married at the time of the interview.)

As the *Transworld* interviewer put it to C.J., "You could have sex with any girl anywhere in the world because of who you are."[4] Although the statement isn't completely accurate, C.J.'s abstinence was not due to a lack of opportunities, thanks to the way our culture views celebrity athletes. And let's face it: There are a lot of hot women on the beaches of the world. But C.J. maintains that life as a pro surfer is not much different temptation-wise from any other walk of life. "There ain't no temptation that I deal with that you don't deal with going to a job that's 9 to 5," he says. "The world's the world whether you're in a square room, or in a bedroom, or in Brazil on the beach."

Since getting married in January 2003, his wife, Rachel, has provided built-in support. "I am accountable to my wife, and she travels with me a lot," C.J. says. "You just don't do things that are gonna make you fall. Don't dance around the fire if you are clumsy and you are going to trip. I try not to put myself in compromising positions."

NEW OUTLOOK

Some of C.J.'s recent lessons have come as a result of him being a new father. His daughter, Genevieve Hobgood, was born July 5, 2005.

"People can tell you how much God loves you, but having a kid, you can see how much God loves you," C.J. says. "You have this human who can't really do anything when she's young, but you love her so, so much. I'm sure when she grows up and she does bad things that I don't agree with, I am still gonna love her so, so much."

The experiences of fatherhood have also given C.J. a new perspective on God. "You can see why we call God the Father," he says.

"He loves us so much no matter what—no matter how bad we are, no matter what we do. It's the same with Genevieve. I can actually realize that from experience. That's kind of where my life's been lately—just realizing God's love for me through my love for my daughter."

Since his championship season, C.J. has remained in the Top 10 surfers in the world. He's a fan favorite and continually ranks high in the annual *Surfer* Poll awards for favorite surfers. His down-home genuineness and good-natured spirit also make him a favorite among his touring pros. But now he is known and respected as much for his spiritual beliefs as for his fearless and powerful riding.

"C.J. and Damien are both constantly bringing up God with all they do," says pro surfer Tim Curran. "With their wins and everything, they are constantly going, 'To God be the glory,' and when I hang out with them, that is what I get."

The swell on C.J.'s horizon looks bright: a red-hot career as one of pro surfing's elite, a legitimate shot at claiming another world championship, the love of a growing family and, most important, a real relationship with his Creator that brings peace and purpose.

Although the rest of us may not necessarily achieve C.J.'s surfing success, he believes that anyone can experience similar spiritual contentment. "Mark my words," he says. "You'll come to a crossroads in your life where you won't have anywhere else to turn. You'll have a decision to make. Everyone goes through it; everyone's human. There will be a time. Give your life to Jesus."

Damo on Ceej

Here's a look at C.J.'s life from the other side, his twin brother, Damien. (Hmm, have they ever entered a contest as each other? That's a question for next time.)

How do you describe C.J.?

As a passionate, strong and loving person. He stands up for what he believes.

Are you more alike or different?

I think more different because I don't get to look at myself, so I just see him. I know when I look at other twins, I trip out, like, Whoa, they are exactly alike, and it's kind of freaky. I can't even tell which one's which. Then, I get an idea of how people think of me and I go, Oh, that's weird.

Do you have any weird twin-sense that people hear about?

Nah, but I do know C.J. well. I know when he is in a bad mood, when he's grumpy, or when I can't even talk to him. But when things happen, he's always going to be right there. We have an understanding that no matter what happens, he'll always be there for me and I'll always be there for him. Even though when we're surfing or doing something together, we want to beat each other really bad.

Out of the Deep

In the beginning God created the heavens and the earth. Now the earth was formless and empty, darkness was over the surface of the deep, and the Spirit of God was hovering over the waters. And God said, "Let the water under the sky be gathered to one place, and let dry ground appear." And it was so. God called the dry ground "land," and the gathered waters he called "seas." And God saw that it was good.

GENESIS 1:1-2,9-10

From the beginning, there was water. The earth may have been formless and empty and dark and silent, but there was water for God's spirit to cover.

Even before the sun and stars, before a flicker of a spark to see by, before a human soul or living organism, there was water. Maybe it was a reflective pool of universal proportions. Maybe it was an unimaginably huge tube peeling through the infinite cosmos, fit only for the Almighty to ride should He so choose. Who knows? Maybe He was testing the earliest physical wave mechanics, giving shape to perfect breakers.

Whatever the ethereal pulse of a forming universe looked like, it was the workshop of spirit. God's spirit was there, hovering, covering, moving above this prehistoric sea, molding it and stirring it

with unequalled divine power, breathing into its molecular structure the ability and force to shape mountains and pulverize rock,
to sculpt terra firma on the grandest scales and to move to the
rhythms of the celestial. One word, one touch from the Creator

The Wonder of Water

- The oceans cover 71 percent of Earth's surface and contain
  97 percent of its water. Less than 1 percent is fresh water,
  and 2 to 3 percent is contained in glaciers and ice caps.
- Earth's longest mountain range is the Mid-Ocean Ridge,
  which winds around the globe from the Arctic Ocean to the
  Atlantic, skirting Africa, Asia and Australia and crossing the
  Pacific to the west coast of North America. It is four times
  longer than the Andes, Rockies and Himalayas combined.
- Ninety percent of all volcanic activity occurs in the oceans.
- Canada has the longest coastline of any country, at
  56,453 miles. That's approximately 15 percent of the
  world's 372,384 miles of coast.
- The highest tides in the world are found at the Bay of
  Fundy, which separates New Brunswick from Nova Scotia.
  At some times of the year, the difference between high
  and low tide is 53 feet, 6 inches—about the equivalent
  of a 3-story building.
- If the ocean's total salt content were dried, it would cover
  the continents to a height of 5 feet.
- At 39 degrees Fahrenheit, the temperature of almost all
  deep oceans is only a few degrees above freezing.[1]

and these waters would be endowed with the punishing power to unleash a chaotic maelstrom on the soon-to-be-formed land and its inhabitants—while also holding the essential force to sustain life and deliver deep joy and serenity to human and animal kind.

Some believe the Creation process occurred in six literal days; others claim that God's days were symbolic time periods in which He shaped and sculpted His masterpiece. Whatever the time frame, it seems reasonable to say that the Creator has always had a special affinity for the great waters. After all, God's second creative move—after forming light and dark—was to separate the waters into earth and beyond, using them to generate a divider called "sky." Then came the seas. As He rolled them back to reveal rising lands and solid shores, He left a liquid blanket over 70 percent of this new planet's surface.

The oceans echo God's calling. Ever moving, always pulsing, sometimes with a soothing, lapping whisper, sometimes with an awe-inspiring roar. The waves beckon, again and again, lurching and rolling, washing in and sucking out, echoing longing, inspiring wonder, stirring a sense of so much more. They elicit a sense of helpless insignificance in the face of vast and widespread power, but offer a connection with the uncontainable. They reveal the existence of unfathomable depths, yet hint at hope of greater understanding.

For millennia, mankind has heard and answered the siren song of the sea. Fishermen, sailors and explorers have navigated its waters; some seeking, some finding—but all responding to a call. Surfers know well the joy of interacting with the living liquid surge. Children are drawn to the thrill of its splash and churn, gleefully letting themselves be swept and tossed by this immensity they cannot begin to comprehend. Even those content to remain on land stand gazing, walking the shores, combing the sands for physical tidbits left behind, while hoping to receive thoughts of renewed clarity and of peace.

Hear the call of the waters and move toward the Caller. Feel the tidal surge and dive in. Abandon yourself in an oceanic vastness and find yourself swept away into the depths of something, Someone, so much bigger.

Where Waves Come From

Waves are a complex phenomenon. People who devote their lives to the study of ocean waves are still discovering things about their formation and the energy they contain. But here are some basics of wave formation that we do understand.

A water wave is the movement of energy through water. Tides are created by the gravitational pull of the moon, but waves are formed by wind blowing over the sea. As the air currents blow across the ocean's surface, they generate friction between the wind and water, transferring energy to the water in the form of ripples, or small waves. The ripples rise above the water's surface just enough to catch more and more wind and grow larger.

Once the ripples have formed, the effects of the wind may have created a difference in sea level between windy areas (such as the Caribbean) and the other side of the ocean (say along western Europe). In order to "flatten out" the sea again, the waves move toward the lowest point. As waves blow out of the higher storm area, the waves with more energy below the ocean surface (longer period waves with greater wavelengths) maintain their strength over distance and become deepwater waves, or a "swell." At this point in their journey, they are nonbreaking waves.

Waves can be predicted and measured using a basic formula with three key elements: fetch length (the area across the ocean over which a wind with a consistent direction generates waves), wind velocity and wind duration. These are used to determine wave height (the vertical distance between a wave's crest and trough) as well as wave periods (the time in seconds between successive wave crests as they pass a stationary point on the ocean surface, such as a buoy).

When a swell continues pushing inland, it eventually hits an obstacle like a beach or reef. It can't move horizontally anymore, so it rises vertically. The swell pushes the wave higher and higher until the wave becomes too tall to support itself and breaks, releasing its energy as it falls onto the beach, reef or rocks. It's at this end of a wave's life that we as surfers experience the exhilaration of the transfer of energy from the wave to our board as it propels us forward on the beautiful ride.

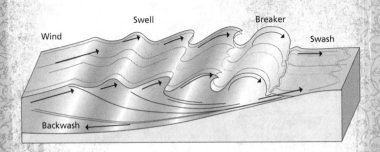

Damien Hobgood: Leading the Charge

Déjà vu. The identical twins were in the water going head to head at First Peak Sebastien Inlet. Although the scene was the same as many a childhood competition for the Hobgoods, the 1,200 spectators lining the beach were a quick reminder that these stakes were much higher. This was the Globe Sebastian Inlet Pro, a four-star event kicking off the 2006 ASP World Qualifying Series.

C.J. launched—literally—to an early lead in the four-man heat. On a long wedging right, the goofyfooter threw a big backside air reverse that scored a 7.50. Damien answered several minutes later, boosting big and landing an inverted, upside-down reverse that the judges awarded an 8.83. The gloves were off.

The twins traded a few more waves. With several minutes left in the 30-minute heat, C.J. mounted his final assault, throwing a towering 360-degree switch and turn. But he slid off his board at the last second and failed to pull in the big points.

At the final horn, Damien stood triumphant, claiming the impressive air-show victory and beating his brother C.J. in a pro heat for the first time. "I was stoked to be battling my brother," Damien says. "We were messing with each other out there, but he got me

Vitals

Born: July 6, 1979

Home: Satellite Beach, Florida

Family: wife, Charlotte

Sponsors: Globe, X-Trak, Fin Control System (FCS), Anon

Big Moments: World Championship Tour victories in Brazil
(2005) and Tavarua (2004)

More: www.hobgoods.com

fired up the way he was surfing. I knew what I needed to do."

Call it high-stakes sibling rivalry. Damien brought home a
$10,000 cash prize, and C.J. pocketed a not-too-shabby $5,000 for
his second-place finish. But what might matter most to the twin
surfing superpowers are brotherly bragging rights.

"He's going to rub this one in, which stinks," C.J. says. "So I've
got to put up with him for a while."

GUNS BLAZING

Damien's win also served notice that he was ready to carry white-
hot momentum into the 2006 World Championship Tour following his career-high No. 4 world ranking in 2005. This was especially impressive, considering he had missed two events due to
shoulder surgery.

Damien has been a formidable threat since reaching the Tour
in 2000. That year, he burst on the scene and claimed Rookie of the

Year honors. The following year, he took the Most Improved Surfer award. Like C.J., Damien has been a perennial fan favorite and Top 10 finisher in the annual *Surfer* Poll awards.

Much of Damien's success has come as a result of his ability to master all of the conditions into which he is thrown. Like his brother, Damien is able to kill it in smaller punt-friendly waves or fearlessly charge monster tubes. "I really admire C.J.'s and Damien's sense of 'no fear,'" Tim Curran says. "They are little bulldog warriors. They love humongous waves, and they never seem to be too intimidated. Sometimes, I'm like, 'Gosh, it's huge. I'm scared,' and they are like, '*Huh?*'"

Damien's performance in 2005 solidified his status as one of the world's elite surfers and left others wondering if he would soon match his brother's world championship. Yet despite all of the success, it was early failure on the road to the top ranks that made the biggest impact in Damien's life, leading him to make an interesting deal with God and eventually form a relationship with Him.

GROM TO GRIND

Damien and C.J. spent their childhood days playing in the ocean at Satellite Beach, Florida, working out their extra dose of sibling rivalry by tiring themselves out in the surf while their mom, Maureen, relaxed and read on the sand. With four kids, she welcomed the breaks. Damien and C.J.'s father, Clifton, had grown up in Oxford, North Carolina, making the four-hour drive to surf Cape Hatteras whenever he could scrounge up enough gas money. It was natural that he would pass on his love for wave riding to his boys.

By 13, Damien and C.J. were serious about their surfing. Kelly Slater was just rising to his unprecedented world domination, stoking the fires of hope for all East Coast grommets. The 'Goods also drew inspiration from rising star Corey Lopez, who was several years ahead on the road to the highest ranks.

The Hobgoods were a religious family. Mom and Dad brought Damien, C.J. and younger sister and brother, Marissa and Travis, to church often enough for them to know about God.

"I was fortunate enough to be raised in a Catholic home and learn about the Bible," Damien says. "Even though I might have not believed it, at least I knew about it."

Damien, along with C.J., hit the World Qualifying Series full-time after graduating from high school in 1998. "It is probably one of the hardest things, traveling around and doing that tour," Damien says. "You have to go to all these lower-ranked [contests] that no one really knows about. No one really notices you. There are, like, 300 people all dog-fighting, and you've gotta have a low seed [to move up]."

They don't call the Qualifying Series "the grind" for no reason. It's a process that Damien says really let him know how well his surfing stacked up against others who were also hopeful of making a living in the waves. It's rare for a surfer to rank high enough on the World Qualifying Series in one year to reach the major leagues of the World Championship Tour. Damien did well, but missed the cut by several spots. He had to watch as his brother graduated to the major leagues and went on without him.

BARGAINING

The twins had always surfed together. They were highly competitive and would offer each other blunt post-heat critiques, but the knowledge that they had each other's backs would always drive them to succeed.

Being left behind was a bummer that fueled Damien's competitive and spiritual fires. "Before that next year, I pretty much made a deal with the Lord," Damien says. "I always knew the Lord was there, but I never had a personal relationship. I was pretty bummed I didn't make it [to the World Championship Tour], and I told the Lord, 'I know You are there, but I know I haven't submitted my life to You. If You get me on the tour, I'll submit my life to You.'"

As the circus of the tour began and the constant traveling and competing ground on, Damien's bold arrangement with God quickly faded from his thinking.

"I remember coming to the end of the year. I was off to Brazil, and I knew [my surfing] was on," Damien says. "The Lord spoke to me, *Hey, you remember that deal we made?* and, I said, 'Yep, Lord, I totally do.' It was basically from that point on that I wanted to live my life for Him. I don't recommend making a deal with the Lord, but . . ." Then Damien laughs.

The path may be somewhat unorthodox, but it is hard to argue with the end result of Damien's spiritual path. In the summer of 2000, he made his commitment to Christ public by being baptized at church.

WHAT IF?

So what would have happened if Damien had not made it off the World Qualifying Series that year? He believes that God would have captured his devotion eventually. Damien's heart was already stirring, and the rising surf star was beginning to question the direction and meaning of his life.

"I thought that making the tour was going to be my happiness," Damien says. "Getting in with these elite surfers, making a name for myself and doing everything that I had dreamed of was going to bring me happiness. But I was kind of already tasting that this isn't real happiness. This is a lot of hard work. You travel most of the year, and you miss a lot of family and friends."

The process lasted about two years. Looking back, Damien says that God was knocking on the door as his view of his life began to shift. "I was seeing the whole world, and seeing how empty all this stuff was—how you can go from contest to contest and big parties with all these people every night," he says. "I could basically go any-where in the world I wanted—the nicest places, the biggest parties with all my friends—and it was still total emptiness."

"It was a really difficult year," Damien continues. "It was like God was saying, *Hey, without Me, you are not gonna be happy. You can only fill the hole in your heart with Me. You are going to try to fill it with all these things, but I am gonna let you know that I'm the only one who can fill that void. When you are ready, I'm here.*"

Damien's upbringing had given him enough knowledge about the Bible to help him recognize the source of his stirrings. "It had gotten to a point where I knew God gave me the gift of surfing, and I knew that I would use it for Him or not," he says. "I thought it was lame that I was just surfing for myself, that it was a selfish thing. The more I kept achieving things, the more empty they were and the more bummed I was."

It was a stark realization to discover that everything he had always hoped for brought no fulfillment. "I thought, *Oh gosh, I put all my eggs—my whole life—into this basket of what I thought was happiness: win-ning and doing good in surfing,*" Damien says. "I was more and more bummed, and I knew that God was the only One who could fix it."

Yet throughout the transformation process, Damien says that there was a battle waging in his mind: "I remember clearly think-ing, *Dude, you know if you give your life to the Lord, no one's gonna like you. You know you're going to be alienated. Most likely no one's gonna want to sponsor you because you're this Christian freak. You are probably not going to have any money because you are not going to have any sponsors. And how are you going to do the tour without money?"*

Damien almost bought into the reasoning. "The devil is probably trying to sell something like that to so many people, and they're buying into it and missing out on so much," he says. "Now I thank the Lord for making that decision. I've experienced the exact opposite of what the devil was trying to tell me."

Supportive sponsors, an unreal career, more money than he thought possible, a beautiful wife, good friends. Damien now enjoys them all with gratitude: "I have blessings beyond my wildest dreams, and I thank God everyday for that. And if it's gone tomorrow, it won't really matter because I don't really put too much value on material things."

PURE 'GOOD

Damien admits that telling some of his friends and industry peers about his newfound belief in Jesus was somewhat awkward, but he tried to simply be himself. "I think people respected that, even if they didn't want to hear the truth," he says. "But [even after becoming a Christian], they still wanted to know me as a person."

Those who do know Damien appreciate his warmth, sincerity, humility and integrity. "Damien is the kind of guy who calls just to encourage you and be sure you're doing well," says Hagan Kelley, associate editor of *Surfing* magazine. "He's kind-hearted. Damien and [his wife] Charlotte are both always looking out for my wife and I. They're really supportive of us and our marriage."

It's those qualities that shape Damien into who he is and guide his interactions with other people. He's not shy about discussing his relationship with the Lord, and he longs for others to experience what he does spiritually. But Damien is not one to force his beliefs on others.

"There are so many fake things and smokescreens in this world," he says. "It's hard to meet someone and really know, Is this person really who he says he is? Is he real? Is he just trying to sell me something? Being Christians and knowing who C.J. and I stand for—that's us. That's what we believe. This is the way it is. People know that's where we are going to come from. We are not going to change with the wind or say this one day and then do something different another day. I think that's a breath of fresh air in the real world. I find that people actually respect me and honor me more than I think they should."

Damien finds it encouraging when friends mention their appreciation for the fact that he doesn't hit them over the head with Christianity. "I think as long as you are the person who you are and you do what God's putting on your heart, He has you where He wants you," he says.

This doesn't mean that Damien always gets it exactly right or always feels completely confident representing Christ. He knows that all humans are going to let each other down sometime. But he draws inspiration from the challenge.

"It's like me surfing. People ask me, 'Do you feel nervous when you are surfing a heat?' And I'm like, 'Heck yeah, I feel nervous.' I feel just as nervous as I did when I was 13 and surfing a contest. That's what makes me perform the way I perform. It's kind of the same way [spiritually]. Sometimes you might feel awkward or nervous, but it heightens your senses and makes you connect with that person on a more heart-to-heart level."

For Damien, it all comes down to being real as a surfer, as a human and as a follower of Jesus. The swells will rise and fall, contest to contest, day to day and relationship to relationship. But, as Damien says, "If the Lord has you where He wants you, He is able to do amazing things."

Ceej on Damo

Here's a look in the mirror from the other half of the pair. (And twin-sense still can be downright freaky!)

How would you describe Damien?

He's a more patient person than I am. He's more book smart than me.

What's the biggest similarity?

Our lives are so similar, even if we don't try. We have a lot of similarities that are kind of freaky. He blows his shoulder out in Tahiti, and then I blow my shoulder out. Same injury. Same arm [left], and it's from surfing. It's like, why does that happen to him and it happened to me, too? Obviously there are twin similarities; those are pretty obvious. And we both love surfing. We both love Jesus.

When you watch Damien surf, do you anticipate what he'll do?

Yeah, that's just from growing up with him my whole life. You can have your best friend or your brother and you just know how he ticks. You just know what moves he's gonna do or what he's going to say before he says it.

How It All Began: A Brief History of Surfing

No one knows exactly when the beautiful art of wave-sliding began. It's commonly accepted that the Polynesians brought an early form of the practice with them when they sailed from Tahiti and discovered the Hawaiian Islands around A.D. 400. A few historians argue that Peruvian fishermen were the first surfers, riding their bundled reed boats to shore as early as 3000 B.C. But no one disputes that the ancient Hawaiians were the first to master stand-up surfing by approximately A.D. 1000.

Captain James Cook and the crews of his ships, HMS *Discovery* and *Resolution*, were the first Europeans to witness the Hawaiian wave-riding way of life in 1778. Lieutenant James King was the first to write about surfing in the ship's journals after observing surfers in Kealakekua Bay on the Kona coast of the Big Island in 1779. He described the Hawaiians as "almost amphibious" and wrote, "They seem to feel a great pleasure in the motion which this Exercise gives."

Men and women, old and young, kings and commoners rode the waves on their hand-carved boards made of *koa* or *wiliwili* wood. During a good swell, entire villages would empty as the inhabitants took to the waves. Surfing was a central part of Hawaiian life and culture, but that way of life would soon take a major blow.

In 1820, Calvinist Christian missionaries from New England arrived on the Hawaiian Islands and were appalled to discover that surfing was not only practiced in the nude but also in mixed company. Although it appears the missionaries didn't directly outlaw the sport, they did frown upon the practice as an immoral waste of time. Their influence essentially shut down the activity.

The missionaries established new regulations encouraging modesty and more work and less play. As the newly Christian Hawaiians attempted to follow the missionaries' spiritual guidance, surfing nearly disappeared. Throughout the rest of the century, surfing became a rarely practiced novelty.

HAWAIIAN RENAISSANCE

At the beginning of the twentieth century, best-selling author Jack London visited Hawaii and was introduced to a group of surfers at the loosely organized Waikiki Swimming Club. Back on the mainland, London wrote an article titled "A Royal Sport: Surfing in Waikiki" in which he described a Hawaiian surfer as "a brown Mercury. His heels are winged, and in them is the swiftness of the sea." The story was published in *The Lady's Home Companion*.

George Freeth was one of the surfers that London met and wrote about. Shortly after London's press coverage, Freeth was invited to California to put on a surf demonstration. At the same time, the Hawaiian Outrigger Canoe Club was established at Waikiki Beach in order to preserve and promote the heritage of surfing. The move kicked off a revitalized interest in the sport.

Several years later, Duke Kahanamoku became surfing's ambassador to the world and the father of modern surfing. The world-record-holding swimmer began giving wave-riding demonstrations in the United States. He became a major celebrity when he won gold in swimming at the 1912 Olympics in Stockholm, Sweden. Eventually, he would also claim Olympic gold in 1920 in Antwerp, Belgium, and silver in 1924 at the Olympics in Paris.

In 1915, Kahanamoku introduced Australia and New Zealand to surfing. And for the next several decades, he promoted surfing around the world.

EARLY RISE

In 1920, 18-year-old Tom Blake met Kahanamoku in Detroit. The following year, Blake moved to Los Angeles and began swimming competitively and surfing. For the next several decades, Blake served as one of the most influential surfers in the world.

Blake created hollow surfboards, which made surfing more accessible to the general public, thanks to the board's lighter weight. He became a commercial board maker and in 1935 was the first to attach a stabilizing fin to a surfboard. Blake also was a founding father of surf photography and writing.

For obvious reasons, the growth and popularity of surfing slowed during World War II. However, the invention of polyurethane foam in the war effort revolutionized board design in the '50s. The lightweight material replaced the heavier wood construction and truly opened surfing to the masses. The decade saw the rise of California surfing hotbeds such as Windandsea and Malibu as well as a host of talented surfers who were developing surfing as a lifestyle.

An Associated Press photo of Buzzy Trent, Woody Brown and George Downing riding a 15-foot wave at Hawaii's Makaha was published worldwide in 1953. Amazed surfers began heading to Hawaii, and riders such as Pat Curren mastered the art of big-wave riding—as well as the scrounging and carefree surf-centric lifestyle. In 1957, Greg Noll led a group of surfers in riding the huge waves of Waimea Bay for the first time.

BOOM AND REVOLUTION

That same year, Bud Browne's *Hawaiian Surf Movies* became the first surfing film, creating a rallying point and communication tool for surfers. But it was Hollywood's 1959 *Gidget* that blew surfing into a national craze.

Suddenly, beaches and surf breaks were packed. Everyone wanted a piece of the surfing life. The Beach Boys, Dick Dale and others brought surf-inspired music to the masses. Hollywood churned out more surf-related movies. Surfware and equipment companies boomed as the public clamored for the beach look. Surfers such as Mickey Dora became pop-culture icons.

Up to this time, surfboards were typically 10 feet or longer in length, but in 1966 Australian Nat Young introduced the world to his revolutionary new shorter board. By 1967, the shortboard revolution was fully underway. The period brought a drastic shift as the climbing, dropping and turning style of shortboarding replaced the noseriding linear approach of longboarding. The '70s, matching the experimental and loosening culture of the hippie era, brought further exploration to riding and board-making styles.

When World Championship contests began in 1964, Australians such as Nat Young dominated competitions. In the '70s, Aussies Peter Townend, Wayne Bartholomew and Mark Richards led the way. The pro surfing era essentially began in 1976 with the establishment of the International Professional Surfers tour, but many surfers were either disinterested or opposed to competition. The International Professional Surfers tour laid the foundation for the surfer as professional athlete, but a revolt in 1982 led to the formation of the Association of Surfing Professionals.

In 1980, Joey Buran became the first California male to win a pro surfing contest. In 1981, the tri-fin Thruster broke on the scene, which gave surfers tighter control. By the middle of the decade, Californian Tom Curren had become an international phenomenon, and his explosive yet fluid new style became the model for all surfers. Surfing enjoyed another popularity boom in the '80s, with clothing companies such as Op, Hobie and Gotcha! capitalizing on the trend.

NEW SCHOOL

If Curren was surfing's first superstar, Kelly Slater was its megastar. Competition remained the centerpiece of surfing in the '90s, and Slater dominated the sport, winning world championships every year from 1993 until his retirement in 1998. During his reign, Slater redefined high-performance surfing and led the New School takeover that brought aerial tailslides to prominence.

Women's surfing took a big leap in the mid-'90s, thanks to Lisa Andersen's star power and talent. She won world championships from 1994 through 1997. Other women, such as Rochelle Ballard, Layne Beachley and Keala Kennelly, also elevated the levels of women's performance as they charged bigger and badder waves. Although surfing remains a male-dominated sport, young girls continue to pick up boards and learn to surf in droves.

The corporate surf industry has flourished in the new millennium, with companies such as Quiksilver, Roxy, Billabong and Hurley leading the way. Wave-riding revenues reached nearly $2.5 billion in 2004. Competitively, Andy Irons reigned in the sport, winning world championships from 2002 to 2004 (although an "unretired" Slater reclaimed the world title in 2005). Live Webcasts have made it easier to watch pro contests, and freesurfing has become a viable professional alternative to the contest circuit.

Riding styles continue to become more dynamic, with surfers pushing new territory and tricks on and above waves. Tow-in surfing has also come of age, thanks to its development by Laird Hamilton, Dave Kalama and others. The strapped version has allowed surfers to ride waves as big as 60 feet, and its practitioners continue pushing bigger all the time.

Surfing will continue to evolve, obliterating old boundaries and forging new ways to experience and interact with wave-riding pleasures. No matter where it goes or grows, we'll all be wise to remember that the huge cultural and economic force known as surfing all comes down to a simple and solitary experience: a man or woman riding a board across the liquid energy of a vast ocean, feeling the stoke all the way.

Skip Frye: Pioneering Surfer and Shaper

In my younger days, surfing was pretty much my god. I think every surfer who is a Christian deals with that. But I found that if I took care of priorities, God would bless my surfing in a most dramatic way—more so than if I put surfing as a priority.

God is faithful. The more I work on my relationship with Him, the more wonderful it is. You can't outgive God. He's blessed me with both surfing and shaping in a capacity where He's given me a platform. I understand that He has blessed me, so I will reflect Him to the surfing public and people around me. That's how I look at it.

It's a matter of priorities. Surfboards and surf can wait. I wake up and try to start each day by saying my prayers, doing my devotions and reading the Good Book. I ask Him to be in my mind and heart and give me wisdom, knowledge and love for the human race as I go about my daily trek, wherever it might take me and whoever I might talk to. My desire is to reflect Him as much as I can.

God uses what you do. My place is just a little garage and shaping room, but He's used it. It's like my little chapel or prayer place. People come here sometimes just to sit down with me. It's quiet, and we have a little prayer time. I've gotten to where I really enjoy it because I see the positive results of it. Every prayer that is offered up, God receives.

God is good, man. That's all I can say. He blows my mind and amazes me. What He does generates more love for Him. I can't talk or praise Him enough for what He's doing and what He's done. Every day is an adventure. It's exciting to watch it go forward. That passion is what He's given me. I can't take credit for anything. My surfing or shaping, it's all the way God has blessed me. I just try to reflect Him and keep that focus: God first.

Chris O'Rourke: Localism Erased

Chris O'Rourke's life was short, but his impact on surfing and on the lives of other surfers lives on today. Chris grew up surfing Windansea in La Jolla, California, and was the ringleader of a crew that enforced a strict and terrorizing localism. By the mid-'70s, Chris was rising through the ranks of the surf world, beating pros when he was only 15. In 1976, Gerry Lopez referred to him as the best California surfer he had ever seen.

But Chris's life was turned upside down when he returned from a surf contest in Australia at 18 years of age and discovered that a lump on his neck was cancerous. He was diagnosed with Hodgkin's disease. During his long, hard fight against cancer, he prayed with his friend Brew Biggs for God to save and forgive him. From that moment on, he started telling everyone from close friends to kids on the beach about Jesus.

Doctors said that Chris would never surf again, but he did. Those who once got a full dose of hardcore localism from Chris now got the message of Jesus. On a flight to Australia, he shared his faith with Joey Buran. Joey didn't immediately give his life to Jesus, but he points to that flight as a divine appointment arranged by God.

The film *Changes* documents what Chris told his sister Lynn in his last days: "These have been the happiest years of my life, since I found Jesus. I really think if I hadn't gotten cancer, I wouldn't have found Jesus. Getting cancer is the best thing that ever happened to me. Before that I was dead and now, even in all this pain, I'm alive. I know the Lord and I know where I'm going."

Chris's pain ended in 1981, and his ashes were scattered by friends and family in the waves at Windansea.

Joey Buran: Original California Kid

The "California Kid" dominated the boys' and juniors' circuits before going pro as a 17-year-old. The goofyfooter became the first California male to win a world pro tour event (Brazil's Waimea 5000 in 1980) and to win the Pipeline Masters in 1984. Joey's seventh place finish that year was his highest on the pro tour and earned him the distinction of being the first Californian to rank in the Top 10. He retired the following year to found and direct the U.S. Pro Tour of Surfing.

In 1987, Joey made the biggest change of his life when he surrendered to Jesus. "I made a verbal confession of faith as a born-again Christian in '83, but my life never matched up," Joey says. "Then in 1987, I read the Gospel of John on my own. The Lord pretty much spoke to me through everything in the book, and by the time I finished, I cast my lot with Jesus."

The once self-described selfish surfer saw big changes. "I broke off an immoral relationship. I didn't really want to go out partying, and I wanted to go to church twice on Sunday," he says. "It was all 'want to', not 'have to.' There was a total transformation within me by the work of the Holy Spirit. I was desiring the things of God's kingdom and making good decisions for the first time."

Joey also knew that God was calling him into full-time ministry. In 1991, he became a pastor in Calvary Chapel churches in the East. In 1996, he returned to California, where he picked up surfing again and became involved in ministry to Orange County surfers and their families. He also claimed victory in the 1998 Masters World Championships (for former pros 36 and older) by charging big right barrels at Mexico's Puerto Escondido.

Joey remains confident that he is serving God in the place where He has put him. "My testimony is that I got saved," Joey says. "God called me out of surfing because He is greater than surfing."

Tom Curren: Icon on a Search

CHAPTER 5

Before there was Kelly, there was Tom.

Before Kelly Slater launched his aerial assault to world domination, Tom Curren claimed an unequalled reign and sparked a revolution that redefined wave riding.

Before Kelly Slater's star shot beyond surfing to captivate mainstream fascination, Tom Curren captured the public's attention, becoming the most popular surfer in the world, even to those who knew little about surfing.

Few have altered the face and soul of surfing as much as Tom Curren. As the Santa Barbara regularfooter rose to dominance in the '80s, his fluid yet powerful style blew minds and revolutionized wave riding. Everyone wanted to surf like Curren.

Yet while the public clamored, the shy surfer remained enigmatic. After winning three world championships, he seemed to lose interest in competition. He drifted off the ASP tour to forge new ground, becoming what amounted to the first professional soul surfer and captivating surfers and fans for years to come, even making a renewed run at the World Championship Tour as recently as 2005.

Vitals

Born: July 3, 1964

Home: Santa Barbara, California

Family: wife, Maki, and sons Frank, Patrick; two children,
Leeann, Nathan, from first marriage

Sponsors: Rip Curl, Channel Islands Surfboards, Island Style

Big Moment: Clinching first world title in classic Bells Beach
heat versus Occy

More: www.tomcurren.com

In spite of, or perhaps because of, Tom's success, the surfing
natural struggled in other parts of his life. Tracing the trajecto-
ries of his public life was difficult for this reluctant icon, and the
tides of his private life that ebbed and flowed through drastic
extremes were difficult for him to grasp. Yet throughout his sto-
ried and mysterious personal life, Tom's path followed a spiritual journey that has led to full-on surrender to Jesus.

BORN TO RIDE

Thomas Roland Curren was born July 3, 1964, to surfing royal-
ty. His father, Pat, was considered the best big-wave rider of the
late '50s and '60s and the era's finest big-wave board craftsman.
He was an original member of the notorious Windansea Surf
Club and among the group that opened the legendary Waimea
Bay to surfing.

Following that epic but wipeout-filled debut, the waterman developed the first specialized big-wave gun, tailor-made to handle big Waimea. Pat became known for his patient wave selection, sometimes waiting hours for just the right wave, and then scoring the biggest and best ride of the day. The intensely quiet charger was known as the King of Waimea.

It came as no surprise, then, that King Curren had young Tom on a surfboard for the first time when he was 2, although Tom didn't begin surfing regularly until the ripe old age of 6.

The family lived in Santa Barbara, California. By Tom's preteen years, he had begun ditching school, running with a bad crowd, drinking and experimenting with drugs. He even ran away from home once. His parents were understandably worried, so Tom's mom, Jeanine, adopted a new approach to supervising her son.

"My mom really stepped in and took care of me more," Tom says. "She quit working and actually got more involved in nurturing me a lot and taking me surfing, picking me up from school and things like that. I'm really grateful she was able to do that. At times I resisted a lot, but in the end because I was at an early age, it was a good strategy."

During that same period, Jeanine encountered Christ and became intense about her new spiritual life. Under her guidance and encouragement, Tom began attending church and youth group in his early teens. At 13, he accepted Jesus. "I was seeing a bigger picture of what things mean and kind of bigger questions," Tom says of his early teen years. "It was a pretty dramatic turnaround."

Surfers owe a great debt to Jeanine Curren. Shortly after she laid down the new law of discipline, young Tom's competitive surfing took off. At 14, his amazing amateur run began with the first of two consecutive boys' division U.S. Surfing Championships.

Two years later, he claimed the juniors' title of the 1980 World Championships, and in 1982, the men's division was also his.

TOUCHING THE FUTURE

Once his amateur goals were accomplished, Tom turned pro shortly before his eighteenth birthday. He promptly won his first event, the Stubbies Pro at California's Trestles, and signed contracts with Op and Rip Curl worth $40,000, an unheard-of sum for a first-year pro.

Tom lit the pro tour on fire and quickly became an international phenomenon. His wave-riding instincts were unparalleled and his natural ability was astounding. It was as if the water was his home environment. His style was unique and inspiring, a blend of dynamic power and graceful fluidity. He invented the "double pump" bottom turn, which provided more speed and power going into off-the-lip moves, and he blended multiple maneuvers with seeming effortlessness.

Almost every young surfer in the '80s and early '90s patterned his or her style after Tom Curren. Even the pros were taking lessons from him.

"His technique was so advanced, it was brilliant," says 1983 and '84 world champion Tom Carroll in a 2005 *Surfing* article. "He really showed me a technique—all of us, the whole world really—and that's when our techniques had to change. Tom came along with this sort of aesthetically complete technique that was a really nice dance on the wave, and the way he shifted his balance and his weight around was really nice, and you could take it on board. So everyone took it on board, I think."[1]

Mark Occilupo, better known as Occy, was perhaps Tom's greatest rival in those days. They will be forever linked in surf history for their classic duels and polar differences: introvert versus extrovert, regularfooter versus goofy, fluid finesse versus raw power, Yank versus Aussie.

Occy recalls his first memory of seeing the then 18-year-old Tom surf during a contest in Australia. "I'd never seen someone have so much fun and make surfing look so good," Occy says. "I remember thinking I just wanted to get *that* good."[2]

NOT *IF* BUT *WHEN*

It didn't take long for Tom to make his mark on pro surfing. He only surfed four of the contests that first year in 1982, winning two and finishing the year ranked No. 19 overall. It seemed inevitable that he would ride his Al Merrick-designed tri-fins to a world title. It was only a matter of time.

That time came two years later at the Rip Curl Pro at Bells Beach Australia. In what is still considered one of the greatest heats in world tour history, Tom outdueled Occy in the semifinals to clinch the 1985 world championship. He was the first American to do so, and at 21, the youngest world champ.

Tom continued to scorch the pro circuit, earning victories at 5 of the first 10 contests of the following season. He claimed his second world title in 1986.

"If you go back to the pre-Slater era, there was no one like Tom Curren," says Joey Buran, 1984 Pipeline Master and tour rival who was considered California's best surfer before Tom rose to the top. "He completely changed pro surfing. His style and his skill were far superior to everyone else's. He did it all at such a young age and at a time when no one thought an American could do anything."

By putting the United States on the surfing map, Tom became a national hero in the surf community and beyond. He had ended the Australian domination of pro surfing. He was young, good looking and humble. *Sports Illustrated* and *Rolling Stone* published profiles of the young star, and every surf video wanted to feature his clips and document his historical rise.

"I think every surfer on the planet was totally inspired by Tom Curren and his style and who he was as a person," pro surfer Tim Curran says. "He was probably one of the most humble surfers ever."

OFF AND ON

The pro tours in the '80s were an unrelenting grind. Contests were held weekly, regardless of conditions. The 1985 season consisted of 21 events.

Perhaps it was burnout. Perhaps it was disinterest. Perhaps it was pressure. Whatever the reason, Tom fell to a fifth-place finish in 1987, and then fifteenth in '88, and then faded off the tour completely in '89. "He could be beat," says Joey Buran. "But usually he beat himself."

In 1990, the 26-year-old apparently decided he didn't want to be beat. He returned to the pro tour, surfing his way through trials events to win his third championship. Along the way, he earned a record-tying seven contest victories in a single season. Between 1982 and 1991, he also set a record, along with Tom Carroll, for the number of consecutive years with a pro contest victory.

Mission accomplished, Tom faded from the tour once again, surfing and winning a few contests in '91. Yet it wasn't as if his surfing was suffering. During the '80s, Tom had joined top pros Tom Carroll and Martin Potter in boycotting the South African contests in an effort to protest the country's racist apartheid policies. Once apartheid lifted in 1991, Tom made the journey to

Jeffrey's Bay for the first time. On his first wave, he connected three legitimate tube rides with more than a half dozen big bottom turn/off-the-lip combos, scoring what *Surfer* magazine called one of the five greatest rides of all time.

But for the most part, Tom spent his days in his adopted home of Anglet, France, with his wife and two young children, creating music and surfing his own isolated breaks.

Still, the world clamored for Tom Curren. In late 1992, Rip Curl signed him to the largest-to-date contract in surf history, worth $2 million. "The Search" was born as the company paid Tom to travel the world, exploring and riding waves wherever he chose, sporting Rip Curl logos.

Tom pushed the boundaries of his own surfing, experimenting with a variety of unusual board shapes and styles, some of which were homemade. This period in Tom's life is widely criticized as one that hindered the development of his natural abilities, but in fact it only added to his eccentric legend. Many held him up as a true soul surfer, willing to color outside the lines and chart his own path in search of the ultimate stoke.

During his competitive prime, Tom had legitimized the fledgling pro surf tour and raised the bar of greatness. (By the time he dropped completely off the tour, he had won a record 33 pro-tour victories. The mark seemed long out of reach until Kelly mounted his own competitive comeback.) Now, by pioneering freesurfing as a financially sustainable way of life, Tom Curren had unwittingly altered the face of surfing once again.

DOWN DEEP

The dance with fame was awkward, and Tom never seemed comfortable following the rhythms of the media. In the water, he was all natural grace and flow, but on shore he mumbled his way through interviews with noticeable discomfort.

While the world hailed him as the savior of surfing and frenzied to catch a piece of him, Tom seemed largely unimpressed, humbly downplaying his status or importance. Perhaps it was the ability of a master who has attained the great heights to which others aspire to grasp clarity of the bigger picture.

At the height of his reign in 1986, Tom told surf journalist Matt George, "There's a lot more than winning a championship. All it signifies is who's best at getting four waves to the beach, and when you look at it in that form, it's really insignificant."[3]

Tom always seemed to know that there was more in life, but remaining in tune with exactly what that was remained elusive throughout his career. Early in his career, Tom told journalist Drew Kampion, "I think He's placed me in surfing because it's my gift. It's what I do. It's what I'm gonna do. And there's a reason for that, I guess."[4] But remaining spiritually centered once he was traveling the world on his own proved to be a difficult challenge.

When Tom was 17, his father left the family, moving to Costa Rica to pursue a remote surf-centric lifestyle. In his teen years, Tom had the spiritual accountability and support of his mother, church and mentors such as Al Merrick, for whom he expresses admiration. Tom knew that he still had support back home, but he admits that he neglected the communication lines and made mistakes as a result. "[My faith] was still there, but I wasn't involved in church and things like that," Tom says. "I was still reading, praying and that sort of thing and trying to keep growing. I didn't go out and surf for God and things like that. I was kind of divided."

Tom's early biblical roots had been strong—strong enough to still offer an indication of Tom's internal condition. "When I found

I was at a place where I wasn't really following [God], I recognized that foundation was eroding," Tom says. "I guess the middle of my touring period was when I sensed inwardly that I was drifting."

The world wanted to know Tom Curren, but it seemed that he was trying to figure out just who he was himself. The process is a common challenge for any young adult, but Tom's path to discovery had the added pressure of public spectacle.

UNDER THE SURFACE

In 1983, the 18-year-old surfer married Marie, a local girl whom he met while surfing in France. The couple made France their permanent home in the late '80s, although Tom's rootless touring lifestyle kept him away from home a great deal. Before long, the couple had two young children.

Though Tom always appeared calm and seemingly unaffected on the outside, on the inside there were storms brewing. You'd never have known it at the time, but Tom later admitted that his professional nemesis, Occy, could really get into his head in those days. But even deeper, there were questions and personal struggles that haunted Tom as well. His quest for answers was coming up empty. "I was interested in psychology and things about the subconscious mind," he says. "I was intellectualizing a lot of things when the need was more spiritual."

Relationally, the Currens' troubled marriage was in shambles by 1993. The couple divorced later that year.

Tom withdrew from the public even more. Yet it seemed that his continued mystique only fueled interest in him. Even as Kelly Slater began his rise to dominance, winning his first world title in 1992, fans seemed just as enamored with Tom. "It was almost as if his sheer inscrutability, his public opacity, was a kind of reflective armor, making it easy for fans to see their projections in him," writes Drew Kampion.[5]

"It would be really hard to be Tom Curren," Joey Buran says. "If people didn't live through it, they can't comprehend it. Tom had so much pressure on him, and he delivered. So he was always in the spotlight."

RECONNECTION

Tom remarried in 1994 to Maki Caicedo of Panama. The couple returned to Santa Barbara, and by 1996, they had two sons of their own, Frank and Patrick.

By this time, Tom began to return to his roots and reconnect with God. At one point in the early '90s, he paid a visit to Joey Buran, who was then a pastor in Virginia. The two had been friends on the pro tour, rooming together on occasion, but they were never close.

"He definitely was empty, and he just wanted to come see me," Joey says. "A couple years later, I saw him and he told me that visit really had a big impact on him, seeing that I could walk away from surfing and live in Virginia and be in ministry and have nothing to do with surfing."

In 1997, the two teamed up for an outreach event at Tom's house in Santa Barbara. About 80 local kids showed up. "He said, 'Just teach the Bible, Joey; just teach something from the Bible,'" Joey says. "And I did, and Tom was so happy he gave away all his surfboards. A couple of kids were looking at boards and were like, 'Dude, this is a cool one.' And Tom was like 'Oh, you can have it.' Then, of course, all these groms are like, 'Dude, can I have a board?' It was like Christmas. It was really cool. I was like, *The Lord really touched him.*"

But Tom still had trouble connecting with a base of local spiritual support. "The problem with Tom is it would be really hard for him to plug into any church," Joey says. "He travels a lot and everyone treats him differently. And Tom always has had a hard time letting people into his world, because people always wanted to take something from him."

Tom experienced renewed spiritual growth, but there were still some dark days ahead that included battles with depression and alcohol. He openly discussed the period in a 2004 *Surfer* interview, saying, "Jesus is there and He's free, and He's all I need. It's something where I know I'm not the only one to struggle with alcohol . . . I'm doing really well at the moment."[6]

COMEBACK

The new millennium began a reemergence for Tom in a number of ways. A longtime musician, he released his first solo album in 2003. The self-titled project received positive reviews and provided a deeply personal and spiritual glimpse of the man who had remained reclusive for so long. Although Tom remained characteristically modest, he agrees that perhaps his music has given him a more comfortable public voice.

In 2005, Tom returned to competitive surfing, making a run at the World Qualifying Series to see if he could earn enough points to reach the World Championship Tour. He received some wildcard spots and invitations to the trials for several Tour events, surfing among the world's top 44, but ultimately failed to earn enough points to make the Tour full-time. Yet though his success was modest, the surf media, pros and fans seemed stoked to see him ripping once again.

Tom doesn't regret the process. "I learned a lot about just how much I want to compete at this time," he says. "I don't really think I have the same drive that I would need to compete with the guys out there. They are really motivated. I had a couple pretty good moments, so I'm happy with that."

The experience was also positive for his family, who supported and traveled with him while his boys were on summer vacation—a contrast to Tom's early traveling days that caused so much strain on his young family. "It was worth doing just because it's something I really enjoy," he says. "It was really quite nice to travel and go with my family."

Don't expect to see Tom claiming another world championship. He says he doesn't have plans for a major competitive run. But he will continue "The Search." In 2004, he re-signed with Rip Curl and will continue his freesurfing, which will undoubtedly garner plenty of video clips and magazine coverage.

Perhaps the greatest hallmark to the comeback of Tom Curren is his newfound sense of contentment, spiritual strength and family stability. "I guess as long as I'm being true to what I need to be is when I find that I have the best results on the outside," Tom says. "Things have been happening good, especially now because of living the life and doing the right thing. And that comes to me from faith, and that is the strength."

Those close to him have seen the differences. "I know he is doing well with his family and with the Lord," Al Merrick says. "I just respect seeing the growth and the changes in him. Knowing him over a long period of time, I see him growing in the Lord and that's wonderful."

"I've seen great progress in his walk with the Lord," Joey Buran says. "Tom has come a long way, and I give him a lot of respect."

As for Tom, he seems to be a man more at peace with himself and his God. These days, he is perhaps more accessible to those still fascinated by his water-borne legend and gratefully aware of the value of all he's discovered. He's taking nothing for granted.

"There's always going to be some kind of struggle, I think, but it's just a process," Tom says. "It's a day-to-day thing."

Keeping the Beat

Many have called Tom Curren an artist in the water. He has long fueled his creative fires on land through music. He began banging the drums as a kid, and then added guitar and bass to his repertoire. In 1993, he recorded his first album, *Ocean Surf Aces*, a good-timing collection that he toured on American coasts with his band, the Skipping Urchins. Through the years, Tom has often performed at surf-industry events, gatherings and contests, and he has shared the stage or jammed with artists such as Jack Johnson, Jackson Browne and Switchfoot. His 2003 release, *Tom Curren*, reached more poignant depths and delivered soulful maturity and stylistic diversity.

Tom regards his music with characteristic humility. "I'm glad to be able to play," he says. "There are a lot of good things that have happened to me with music. Hopefully my songs will get better. I'd like to write a good song or something, but you want to just kind of say what you feel. It's a matter of whether you really feel what you're singing about. And that's kind of a mystery how that works. It's nice at times when it feels like it's working, but it's hard to get in that zone."

"I'm under no illusion of being some personality for the fame," Tom adds. "I have a better time and enjoy more gospel kind of music anyway. It's kind of what I like playing. I think the message is really the most important thing. I think my style is pretty simple and the message is simple enough—entertaining, but not just entertaining."

Taking Shape: A Brief History of the Board

"I've been shaping boards for more than 35 years," says surfboard designer John Carper in the 2004 film *Noah's Arc*. "I've shaped— I don't know how many; I stopped counting because it was making me feel old—well over 50,000 surfboards by hand.

"I was a sculpture major in college. I don't look at people as being different; I look at them as really different. When I look at anybody, I block them off. I see the shapes in their bodies and in their faces. That's what I do with surfboards as well.

"When we make a board, we have a plan. The board is designed for a specific use. When I make a 10-foot P.B.U. [Pray Before Use model] board, it's meant to ride a 30-foot or 20-foot wave. It won't ride a 2-foot wave. Each one of these boards is a unique board for a specific job.

"When you look at the outside of a surfboard, you can probably tell pretty much what it's for. To know your purpose and what you're designed for, a person has to look at the inside of themselves.

Because even though people might look different on the outside, it's all about what goes on inside."[1]

SHAPING HISTORY

The ancient Hawaiians handcrafted their surfboards from mighty native trees, reserving the biggest for royalty. These *olo*, as they were called, could be as long as 24 feet and weigh up to 200 pounds. Good thing they didn't have to hoist them onto roof racks.

The early boards of the twentieth century were handcrafted in much the same way as those of the early Hawaiians. A surfer usually crafted the finless solid wood planks in his backyard or carriage house. Redwood was the tree of choice.

Hollow boards became popular in the 1930s and '40s. Although still made of wood, the lighter "cigar boxes" weighed about 45 pounds—and were much easier for aspiring surfers to transport than the 70-pound solid planks.

American chemists developed polyurethane foam during World War II, and in the '50s, Santa Monica surfer Dave Sweet began experimenting with the material for surfboards. By the late '50s, foam blanks were the core material of choice for surfboards, providing a cheap and plentiful replacement for balsa wood. The switch signaled the most important technological breakthrough in surfboard history.

The new lighter-weight boards made surfing more accessible to the masses. Now, even kids could drag a 10-foot, 25-pound board into the whitewash for an afternoon of fun.

The introduction of Nat Young's new shortboard, "Sam," at the 1966 World Contest in San Diego signaled the beginning of the shortboard revolution. In the following years, average board length dropped from 10 feet or more into the 7-foot range. The more maneuverable designs also made it possible for surfers to access new sections of waves and create moves never before dreamed of.

In the early years of the new millennium, surfers enjoy more board varieties than ever. Top riders and even many recreational surfers own and use a quiver, an array of board shapes and lengths that allows them to choose a ride customized for a particular type of wave. Fins can be attached and detached at will, allowing for different types, sizes and arrangements that alter the "steerability" of a board.

Board materials continue to evolve as well. December 2005 brought the shutdown of Clark Foam, a company that supplied 80 percent of foam blanks to American shapers. The post-Clark era will no doubt bring more openness to the use of different and creative materials such as epoxy resins and extruded polystyrenes.

SHAPING STEPS

Surfboard materials have changed most significantly. Designs have evolved. And since the 1990s, computer-programmed machines have taken over the process of cutting blanks—streamlining production and allowing more systematic and precise fine-tuning of styles. But overall, the processes of creating a surfboard have remained largely unchanged since the 1950s.

Each shaper has his own way of working, but generally, each takes a foam blank through a basic six-step progression. First is "skinning," a process of using a power planer to bring the blank to within ⅛ of an inch of its desired shape. Next, the shaper traces template forms, or patterns, drawing the final shape onto the foam. He then cuts the board's outline with a saw or router and squares off the rails, or edges, with rough-grit sandpaper. With the board bottom-up, he planes and sands to set the rocker, or curve, from nose to tail. More sanding and planing follow on the top. Fine-tuning the entire board comes next. Finally, a shaper uses progressively finer sandpaper to blend and even out all bumps or ridges. When the shaper's work is done, the board is ready for fiberglassing.

Next comes any artwork, which is usually added by airbrushing. "Glassing" usually refers to the entire post-shaping process, but it includes a few different steps. First comes laminating, enveloping the blank in fiberglass by covering it with a sheet of fiberglass and spreading over it with a resin catalyst. Hot coating, or sand coating, comes next. A second coat of resin is brushed on. As it dries, a wax-based sanding agent rises, creating an easy-to-sand surface. Fins or fin boxes are added once the hot coat dries, and then the board is sanded.

Longboards are usually gloss coated with a third coat of resin, which provides a lustrous shine when sanded. Most shortboards are complete after the hot-coat sand, as the extra ounces of an additional coat can alter performance.

KEY SHAPES

Longboard. Originally all boards were long, but the term "longboard" arose in the late-'60s-era shortboard revolution to distinguish the blunt-nosed 9-foot-and-up vehicles. The '80s brought an explosive return to smooth-styled longboard riding. Longboards remain the board of choice and necessity for beginners.

Hollow. First created by Tom Blake, these wooden hollow boards (also called "cigar boxes") were popular in the 1930s and '40s. The hollow centers meant less weight, which made the 45-pounders—and surfing—more accessible to more people.

Hot Curl. This finless board was popular in the 1930s and '40s, but was used mainly in Hawaii. The shortened, narrowed tails made these 65-pounders the first specialized big-wave boards.

Malibu Chip. These balsa-core boards, built in the late 1940s and early '50s, were generally about 10-feet long and weighed about 25 pounds. Bob Simmons's versions were the first to incorporate principles of nose-lift, foil and precision rails.

Pig. Dale Velzy's '50s version of the Malibu chip is considered the prototype of the modern longboard. Pig riders such as Dewey Webber invented "hotdog" surfing, the tricky, expressive style that featured multiple board turns and body positions.

Gun. Originally called big-wave guns, these streamlined boards ranging from 10 to 12 feet are designed for paddling into waves 20-feet and up.

Hybrid. These medium-sized, full-figured "funboards" fall in the 8-foot range and provide a balance between stability and maneuverability. They are popular among beginners, intermediates and older surfers. Specific variations include the "egg" and "mini-log."

Fish. Featuring stumpy, blunt-nosed, split-tailed, twin-finned boards, the fish was invented in 1967 and used for creativity and speed on small waves.

Tri-fin. Australian Simon Anderson's 1981 Thruster model was the first board to use three equal-sized fins in triangle formation. The design was immediately and widely copied, and the tri-fin remains the high-performance board type of choice today, thanks to its superior maneuverability.

Tow Board. These shortboards (generally 5 feet, 6 inches in length to 6 feet, 6 inches in length) appeared in the early 1990s and are fitted with foot straps that allow a rider to be towed behind a Wave-Runner into giant surf—20 feet, 40 feet, 60 feet, or more.

John Carper, JC Hawaii

I was one of those guys who came kicking and screaming into the whole Christian thing. And really, a lot of my ministry is for people like me. We're basically ministering to unchurched people on the North Shore. They may never go into a church their whole lives. They may be as close as they get by coming and eating some food at our house and listening to Christian music and hanging out with Christians. But our goal is to get them into local churches.

I know these people because I was one of them. They are the guys who sit in the back when you do get them to church. They never help. When the basket goes by, they don't even drop in a quarter. The rest of the week, they don't want to look like they know you. But God loves these guys even though they are not going to come in the front door. I still have that in me. I never get into arguing with people because I see myself too much in them. I've had people who literally wanted to fight and a couple days later those guys accepted the Lord. I can totally relate to that.

I'm a full-on born-again Christian. But I try to keep it real and remember where I came from. I don't like that worldly stuff anymore, but I remember how much I loved it and why. Fortunately for me in my areas of ministry, there is a pretty big "cool" factor that goes along with being a shaper. I see that and am aware of that and I use that.

I try to keep my relationship real with Jesus so that I'm growing and understanding and doing. I stumble constantly. I'm not saying I have a great influence on every person I meet. I feel overwhelmed that I *don't* seem to have an influence on most people I meet. But I guess I'm considered a token Christian in the surf world, and I don't mind being that. I just try to make Him a part of my life that is always evident.

Eric Arakawa, Hawaiian Island Creations

I do what I do because I love to surf. But building boards and surfing is a means to an end. God speaks to me while I work, but He speaks to me all the time. I just have to have my ears open.

I actually tried to get out of building boards for a long time. I was trying to get into some other aspect of the industry. I grew up with this stigma that surfers are bums, and it stuck with me. There are many achievers in my family—engineers and teachers and doctors and dentists—so I always felt I needed to get a "real" job.

For a while, I was trying to become someone else, and I got caught up more in seeking the favor of men than seeking the favor of God. But I realized that God wants me to bloom right where He planted me. He created me for a specific purpose. So building boards and surfing is a means to an end—it's to fulfill my purpose in Him that I may reach someone with the gospel.

I have a whole different outlook on this business and what I do in the industry, and I enjoy it. I come to work and look forward to what God has and how He's going to use me. I feel really blessed to be in this industry, especially here in Hawaii. I know that God has me in this position to be His ambassador. It's awesome.

In the past, I put down the whole profession, joking about how I build beach toys. But I've felt God saying, *You know what? You're doing this for Me. I've called you.* So I'm careful now and don't take it lightly, because it's not what I do for work; it's what I do for the King. It's my calling. I've been called by the King of kings to serve Him, and I don't want to insult the King. It is a high calling.

Al Merrick: The Shape of Legends

The master is in his element. A visible layer of polyurethane foam dust coats his 3M respirator mask, scruffy gray-flecked beard, Channel Islands cap and T-shirt, baggy shorts, sandals—and all the skin in between. He moves intently around the center of this simple, blue, 8-by-10-foot room. Tacked on the walls are a few faded surf magazine spreads with corners curling and some board-order forms with notes and measurements for the likes of Rob Machado and Dane Reynolds. Hand planers, sanders, templates and various other tools are scattered about on shelves and in corners. Every square inch is covered in dust.

The door is open, but the shaper is oblivious to the world outside. On a padded sawhorse-like stand lies a polyurethane foam blank, the inner core of a surfboard in the making. The artisan circles, stroking his creation with a sheet of sandpaper backed with egg-crate padding. Again and again he works the surface as soft foam yields to the coarse grit of sandpaper. A file comes out for more bite as the craftsman works a rail. A hand-planer cuts a deeper groove to remove volume. Occasionally, headphones go on while the sound of a power sander whirs.

Vitals

Born: March 11, 1944

Home: Santa Barbara, California

Family: wife, Terry, and children Britt and Heidi

Team Riders: Kelly Slater, Rob Machado, Dane Reynolds, Tom
  Curren, Taylor Knox, Tim Curran, Bobby Martinez, Kalani Robb,
  Sofia Mulanovich, Rochelle Ballard, Lisa Anderson, and others

Big Moment: Shaping more than 70,000 boards; supplying
  boards to six world champion riders

More: www.cisurfboards.com

The man's motion is constant and smooth as he turns the
board and works the board, now lifting it to peer intently down the
rail, now brushing off its coating of dust and running his finger-
tips across its surface. Each movement has purpose.

"Are you working by feel?" I ask.

"Yes, and by sight," Al Merrick answers, remaining focused on
the board. It is a retro Tom Curren squash, a classic style now due
for an update.

Just outside the shaping chamber, an '80s-era original squash
tail leans nearby for reference. Artifacts of conquests past accom-
pany it and line the walls. Boards lean together, tagged with the
names of surf icons: Kelly Slater, Taylor Knox, Lisa Andersen,
Rochelle Ballard, Sofia Mulanovich, "Skindog" Collins, Joe Curren,
and more. These are sticks well loved, most past their prime. They
may be dinged a bit and slightly yellowed in some cases, but their

concaves and tails still stand sentinel, providing guidance and communicating the intricacies of their designs when placed in the hands of the master. Now they are guides to the new and evolving styles.

Al Merrick's factory may be a shrine to great surfers past and present, but don't get the wrong idea. This is no museum with climate-controlled vaults and glassed-in displays. This is a shaping shop where dust lines the floors and walls. Stairs leading through the labyrinth are bare plywood. This has been Al's headquarters since the '70s, and rooms and doors are makeshift, added through the expansions of the decades. Approximately 3,000 blanks jam the larger storage rooms, although the supply is less during my second visit following the infamous Clark Foam shutdown. This may just be the leading surfboard factory in the world. And it's all about function.

Al Merrick has created some masterpieces through the years. Some surfers admire the high-performance lines of his Flyer or Black Beauty more than the brushstrokes of a Monet or Picasso painting. But Al considers himself a craftsman or a designer, not an artist.

Whatever title they use, hordes of surfers are willing to pay top dollar for Al's work. And it's not at all uncommon for top pros to order a quiver of "Als" at some point in their career. It can't hurt that the two most dominant competitive surfers of all time, Kelly Slater and Tom Curren, rode Merricks to their amazing string of world championships.

Al Merrick could be a proud and arrogant man, boastful of his surfboard kingdom. He could credit his success to his hard work and lay claim to the skills he has honed for more than 35 years. Some wouldn't blame him if he carried a sense of entitlement or even retired to enjoy the material possessions with which he's been rewarded. Instead, Al Merrick conveys humility.

"The only thing I can attribute [my success] to is God," Al says. "I've been blessed to be able to work with some of the top guys in the world, and obviously that means a lot. But that's not due to anything special I have."

BIRTH

In one sense, Al Merrick is an elder statesman, a respected leader in the surfing tribe. Yet as much as he is an esteemed sage, he is a powerful chief, ruling at his prime.

Al has a deep passion for his craft, and he's not letting anything slide. There are nights when he awakens with a new shaping idea: an adjustment to the vee, a little more taper to the rails, the link to infuse a retro classic with modern knowledge. Much of the man's conscious and unconscious thought is spent on creating and innovating board designs.

When Al watches surfers live or on video, he's seeing much more than sick airs or insane tail slides. "A lot of times I'm looking at how the water's releasing off the board, or where the board is catching, or what could make it turn a little tighter in that particular section," he says.

It was a natural progression for Al, a good surfer in his own right, to go from riding to shaping surfboards. He says he's always been interested in how things work, and in his early days he built boats as well as boards. Al began toying with his own shapes after Australian Bob McTavish introduced his shortboard experiments to California in the late '60s. Al began as a backyard shaper in 1969, selling boards to local stores under the Channel Islands Surfboards name.

"Somewhere it switched for me from going out and surfing my own boards to designing around guys who were better surfers than I was, and then on to world-class surfers way beyond my ability," Al says. "Somehow it switched from being just for my own gratification, making a board for myself, to [its] being for someone else and watching them surf it."

REBIRTH

During the hippie era of the '60s and '70s, Al experimented heavily with drugs, until he was busted by the cops. After a drawn-out legal process that included one hung jury and a retrial, he served eight months behind bars.

"I was just in a downward spiral there," Al says.

It was his lowest point, and the one that led him to God. While Al was detained, a friend visited his cell to tell him about Jesus. The message of forgiveness clicked, and Al handed over control of his life to Jesus.

Ironically, jail provided the new believer his first taste of freedom. There, he began to study the Bible and experience fellowship with other believing inmates. The growth process solidified his choice to live in a living relationship with his Creator.

Previously, Al had been involved in Eastern religious practices of Self Realization Fellowship, especially meditation, in an effort to achieve an inwardly focused sense of God-consciousness. But once he ran into trouble with the law, Al felt abandoned by the group. "They didn't send any literature or anything," Al says. "They didn't support me at all. [It was like,] 'When you get out of jail, we can talk to you again—maybe.'"

It was a stark contrast to what Al experienced from Christians and his newfound Savior. "Christ was always there with me," he says. "That was always really the distinction in my mind: They [my old friends] are gone, but here is the Lord."

IT'S NOT WHO YOU KNOW; IT'S HOW YOU TREAT THEM

In one sense, Al has been defined by his relationships, especially those with world champion surfers. He first came to prominence shaping boards for 1977 world champion Shaun Tomson. In the '80s, it was Tom Curren, as well women's 1983 champ Kim Mearig. Four-time women's champion Lisa Andersen (1994-97) rode Merricks, as did Kelly Slater throughout his domination of the '90s and the new millennium.

No one can question the unparalleled mastery of Tom Curren and Kelly Slater. It's no wonder they have been some of Al's favorites to work with.

"The object is always to catch up to where they are in their imagination as surfers, where they can imagine themselves going on a wave," Al explains. "I'm always trying to catch up and make boards that allow them to go there. That makes it interesting for me. It makes me more excited about making boards for them to be able to help their surfing improve. But I get just as excited about shaping boards for my friends or local guys."

Perhaps it was Al's early lessons in relationships that helped shape him into the genuinely caring person that he is. He doesn't come across as an extrovert who thrives on knowing and connecting with as many people as possible, but he seems genuinely interested in others, friendly and welcoming. Basically, he comes across as laid-back and down to earth.

"He grasped what was going on with design changes in the early '80s and translated that well into boards and designs through those years and up to the present," says Tom Curren. "It's something that demands respect. He's pretty humble about it, and I think that's one of the reasons why people respect him even more."

Al's expertise has carried him to the top of the surfing industry, but it's the relational quality of his work that has drawn perhaps the highest praise from his celebrity-status colleagues.

"We've connected on so many levels over the past 16 years—he's a second dad to me," überchampion Kelly Slater told *Surfing* magazine in 2005. "I wouldn't be where I am today without him."[1]

"We hardly spend any time on the technical stuff—he figures that out right away," pro Taylor Knox said in the same *Surfing* article. "My relationship with Al is more personal: a lot of conversations about family, love and life go into every one of my boards."[2]

And prayer. Most of Al's time goes to shaping the boards for his A-list team riders. As he works, he often prays for the board's recipient. "If someone I'm making a board for doesn't know the Lord, I pray that they would. I pray about problems in his or her life. It's not like I'm praying over this board to be magic. I pray for the people that God would move in their lives."

It's well known that Al played an important role in Tom Curren's life, sponsoring and guiding the prodigy from his early teen years. Tom says he considers Al a spiritual mentor for whom he holds a great respect. "He's a good example," says Tom. "He's had a lot of success, but it hasn't changed him. I think that has to do with his faith and beliefs. He's given me good advice, and he is somebody I admire."

Tim Curran hasn't worked with Al nearly as long, but he has picked up Al's wisdom along with excellent boards. "He's got that father- or grandpa-figure style that you're just drawn toward," Tim says. "I know he's been that way for a long time and for many surfers."

Praise and respect come not only from team riders but also from industry peers.

When I ask esteemed shaper John Carper of JC Hawaii about fellow believers and competitors Al Merrick and Eric Arakawa, he answers, "I respect them as fellow warriors. We go in the pit and draw our swords in competition. I'm happy to even be included in the same breath as those guys. I'm being a little facetious about the warrior stuff, but they are awesome brothers. We're all fighting on the same team when it comes down to it."

FINE-TUNED

It's Al's final products that have made his name famous. It's the willingness to listen to his riders that has fueled his give-and-take process of subtle refinement. The top-level input combined with Al's intricate understanding of fluid dynamics has proven to be a fail-proof formula.

In his characteristic humility, Al points out that his style is to build on and fine-tune the creations and discoveries of others. "I'm not out there making new technologies. I'm using them," he says. "There are people out there, the mad scientists, who dream up new technologies, new ways to make boards. I'm kind of the guy who will bring it in and see if it works, test it out. In the meantime, I'm just trying to improve what I'm doing."

There are good reasons why the "mad scientists" keep coming to Al with their new ideas and discoveries. His refining style has allowed him to dial in good designs to perfection and popularity. For example, Australian Simon Anderson first introduced the tri-fin Thruster in 1981, but it was Al's fine-tuning that made the tri-fin the universal board of choice by the mid-'80s. (Of course, it didn't hurt that he was developing that style with Tom Curren during Curren's rise to superstar status.)

Don't think that because Al chooses to synthesize slowly and subtly that he is set in his ways. He has actually remained on the forefront of shaping innovation even when his choices haven't been completely popular at the start. In the early '90s, Al was one of the first shapers to implement the use of foam blanks cut by computer-programmed machines. Even though each board was still hand-finished, many at the time considered the move surfing blasphemy. Now it's common practice.

"Computer pre-shapes allow the surfer to get the closest possible board to my designs," Al says. Because each board is begun from a standardized blank, cut to specific pre-set measurements, Al or his other shapers can sand, trim and fine-tune finished boards with greater consistency.

"The real beauty of using the machine is that a board I develop for Kelly [Slater], Rob [Machado] or Taylor [Knox] can be expanded or contracted to work for surfers of different sizes and abilities," Al explains. "Before the computer, doing this would have been impossible."

Even before the momentous Clark Foam shutdown at the end of 2005, Al was experimenting with different materials such as styrofoam, epoxy resins and hollow Salomon blanks. He has even created several board styles using durable Tuflite, an aerospace epoxy technology based on an expanded polystyrene (EPS) core.

It's Al's ability to work with an eye to the future that has made him disinterested at times in revisiting board designs of the past. But his ear for his riders' desires and input rules. When creative style masters Rob Machado and Dan Malloy kept requesting retro boards such as a fish and a single fin, Al was reluctant. The boards had been done 30 years ago. But as the riders persisted, Al decided to give it a go. The result was a pair of stoked pros who love experimental surfing, a satisfied shaper who discovered new pleasure from infusing new ideas into old shapes, and a beneficiary populace of surfers who benefit from the ability to purchase the results in the form of the smooth, fast-riding CI Fish or MSF and MSFG^2 single fin boards.

Al's continued work with Tom Curren has yielded similar results, making available to the public a replica of the famous Black Beauty and its updated Red Beauty version. Some of Al's latest tinkerings have been with stand-up paddleboards, ancient Hawaiian inspired 12- to 20-foot boards steered by dragging and dipping a long oar in a breaking wave.

A GIFT

How does one stay passionate about his work for nearly four decades?

"I don't think you lose your passion for the ocean," Al answers. Throughout his 40s and early 50s, Al remained an avid surfer, going out no matter what the conditions: windswell, fog—it didn't matter. Now the Rincon local who says he's worn out his body is more selective, waiting for sunny, glassy conditions.

"I make toys. People have fun," Al says. "Probably my favorite part is making something that works. I make it and a guy goes out and rides it and says, 'This is a great board.' That's my favorite part."

You could say Al is just a conduit of sharing the stoke, the wisdom, the love—and more. "I've just been given a gift in the area of designing and shaping," he says. "But even more, I've been given the gift of mercies from God to be able to do what I do and have everything come together. The whole thing is a gift."

A gift that Al Merrick continues to pass on.

No One's Perfect

"Oh yeah, I do [make mistakes]. I just made one on this board that I'm trying to correct now [for Kelly Slater]," Al answers when I ask about errors.

"I've lost it before and broken boards on the rack—just karate chopped 'em, which feels pretty good after you've made a mistake. Just break it in half and throw it in the trash can. Generally I come back around, but it sort of releases the pressure.

"I may be off track for months or weeks on boards. I keep a lot of records, so I backtrack to see where I might have gotten off a little bit. Because my mind is always toward design and improvement, maybe I've tried putting something in a board that I thought would improve it, and then get six months down the road and realize, *Oh, my gosh, that wasn't an improvement; it's causing problems.* So I've got to backtrack."

Once You're In, You're In

It's the shakka on the side of the road, the "Howzit" in the Hawaiian parking lot, the hoot from the shoulder, the stoke that spreads from coast to coast.

No matter where you go, surfing is a brother- or sisterhood. Surfers are a family, a community sharing a love and a lifestyle. As Kelly Slater put it in the film *Step into Liquid*, "You're done. Once you go surfing you're in. It's like the Mob or something. You're not getting out."[1]

Sure, everyone loves deserted breaks and secret spots, but it's the rare Jeff Clark who can surf a Mavericks all alone for years at a time. Even Clark tried to get others to join him. The thing is, most of us want the uncrowded breaks—to share with our buddies. We want them to see our sick laybacks or deep pigdogs. We want the guys or girls to feel the exhaustion and relive the moments of an epic session.

That's because surfing is communal—and has been since the beginning. The Hawaiians hit the waves together. The forefathers of modern surfing gathered to ride in clubs. They may have thumbed their noses at the rules of mainstream society, but they

Core Community

Christian Surfers International (CSI) is about surfers reaching surfers with a relevant message about Christ and serving others through relationships. The ministry was birthed in the late '70s by a group of Australian teenagers with a vision for reaching out to fellow surfers. And after holding three international conferences, CSI went from being a casual network to an international mission movement. The organization crossed to America in 1984 when Christian Surfers United States began in Santa Barbara, California.

"We have a passion for Jesus, a passion for surfing and a passion for our world surfing communities," the CSI mission statement reads. "Combined, this makes for a worldwide family of individuals and mission groups who are dedicated to reaching the world surfing community for Jesus."

"Christian Surfers is a long-term missions ministry," says Chandler Brownlee, director for Christian Surfers United States. "We do send some short-term missions teams out of the country, but for the most part, our local chapters are long-term missions for people who live and surf and go to church in our backyards."

Basically, the group views itself as a bridge between the beach and the church. And those bridges exist in local chapters of countries around the world. Most countries have leaders from nearby churches involved in their efforts. The local programs typically feature outreaches that include surfer-friendly Bible studies, contests, camps, coaching, day trips, or special events. And the branches from different nations often partner. Christian Surfers United States published a new *Surfers New Testament* in partnership with Aaron Chang's Living Light Media, and the Australian office has printed and translated the original *Surfers Bible* into several different languages.

thumbed their noses together. They were forging a lifestyle, and there was unity in their pursuit for a better way of waves.

Yes, localism has always raised its ugly head and brought its own brand of dark-hearted surf culture. It's just human nature to get greedy about a good thing, especially when that good thing comes in limited quantities. But even localism reveals the fraternal spirit of the surf. It takes numbers to enforce mob rule. One man cannot possess a beach break alone.

More often than not, the joy of riding the raw energy of the sea draws us together.

Activities give us common bonds, no matter what they are. Clubs and societies are built around pursuits of all sorts based on ideas, beliefs, games and hobbies. But few represent as strong a subculture as surfing. "Becoming a competent surfer actually does bear a resemblance to joining some rigorous cult," writes William Finnegan in the foreword to *The Encyclopedia of Surfing*.[2]

As surfers, we are honored to be drawn into the cosmic dance, touched by universal forces such as celestial tides and unseen gales, and gifted with the momentary bliss of playing among heavenly forces. To know that we have experienced such wonders leaves us with appreciation and thankfulness, whether we can articulate it or not. To encounter another human who shares such awe is to tear down surface walls and connect on a deeper level.

Surfing has been built as a lifestyle. Some pursue it with religious fervor. Others dabble. Some are able to make a living doing it. Others stick to recreational status. But all understand *that* feeling of riding a wave and what it's like to hear the call to come back for more.

"There is that unspoken bond no matter where you go around the world with surfing," Matt Beacham says. "We all enjoy this beautiful sport. When you add the Christian element to that, you are talking about a definite bonding experience."

Wahine's World

Surfing is often thought of as a predominantly male sport, but women have had a strong presence in the community since the time of the ancient Hawaiians. Recorded images of Polynesian women surfers were captured in etchings by famed author Mark Twain as early as 1819. Women have been surfing in California since the 1920s, and the first Australian to ride a surfboard was a woman: Isabel Letham, who rode tandem with Duke Kahanamoku when he intro-duced Australians to board riding in 1915.

Other women, such as Mary Ann Hawkins in the '30s and '40s, Linda Benson and Joyce Hoffman in the '50s and '60s, Margo Oberg in the '70s and '80s, and Lisa Andersen and Layne Beachley in the '90s, have paved the way for today's top competitors.

While the surf-industry image of females has been heavily influenced by the media portrayal of women as sexualized "bikini babes," times are changing. Today, numerous profes-sional female surfers endorse the sport's products and tour on the ASP women's World Championship Tour. Today's top competitors, including Megan Abubo of Hawaii, Sofia Mulanovich of Peru, and Chelsea Georgeson of Australia, are just as intense as male surfers, capable of the most difficult maneuvers, and bring their own spirit to the water.

Within this group stands a community of women who love surfing and embrace Jesus. They stand counter to the culture of sex and ego that can dominate the surf world.

Hawaiian-born Sanoe Lake is one who isn't impressed by awards, fame or material wealth. In a *Transworld Surf* article, she says, "Of all the great lives I've studied, the life of Jesus Christ has been the one that's impressed me above and beyond any other in the history of mankind."[3]

Shannon McIntyre has her hands in just about every aspect of surfing. A rider, shaper, artist and avid surf traveler, she clearly loves surfing. But all that comes second to her relationship with Christ. "I love Jesus and look to Him for inspiration in every part of my life," she says. "He is the Lord and was a punk-vagabond with His revolutionary love and healing message that through Him we can have a personal relationship with God. My life has been supernaturally blessed ever since I accepted the gift of God's love for me. I give props and praise to God in everything I do, because all good gifts and talents are from the Lord."[4]

Without a doubt, the swell of women's wave riding is growing and getting stronger every day.

Bethany Hamilton: Surfing's Survivor

The news rocked the surfing community and sent tsunami-sized shock waves around the world. *Shark attack! Hawaii.* You probably remember hearing the headlines.

A wiry, carefree teenaged girl had been out on dawn patrol to scavenge a few good rides on an unimpressive day. Tunnels, located on the North Shore of Kauai, was pretty flat, but it was a beautiful morning, and she was glad to be in the water.

The session had been uneventful for about 30 minutes. The lineup was uncrowded. Yet it would only take an instant for the idyllic scene to shatter, forever changing young Bethany Hamilton's life.

Bethany sat waiting near her best friend, Alana Blanchard, and Alana's dad and brother. Out of nowhere a 15-foot, 1,500 pound tiger shark raised its menacing head out of the water and took a 16-inch bite from Bethany's board, removing her left arm just below the shoulder. Bethany never saw it coming.

"You would think having your arm bitten off would really hurt," Bethany later wrote in her autobiography, *Soul Surfer*. "But there was no pain at the time."[1] Just pressure and tugging.

Vitals

Born: February 8, 1990

Home: Princeville, Hawaii

Family: mom, dad, and brothers Noah and Timmy

Sponsors: Rip Curl, Subway, Jamba Juice, Volvo, Claire's

Big Moment: Tearfully standing to surf again on November 26, 2003, as friends and family looked on at a secret spot

More: www.bethanyhamilton.com

Bethany never screamed. She simply told Alana, "I just got attacked by a shark," and began paddling for shore. Alana's dad helped push Bethany to the beach, while Alana's brother paddled ahead to call 911. Fellow surfers, beachcombers and eventually paramedics and doctors soon mounted a rescue effort.

Who could predict the widespread attention and concern that immediately began pouring in from across the nation and from continents far away? Shark attacks are always big news. Evening news anchors eat up the sensational and traumatic reports of unsuspecting surfers or swimmers enjoying the ocean one minute and then suddenly becoming unsuspecting prey to the beasts of the deep.

Bethany's story began as no exception. With her survival uncertain and an island-wide rescue effort underway, news spread instantly after the attack. People around the world prayed. Even those who didn't know her asked God to save the life of "that surfer girl who got attacked by a shark," and let out a sigh of thanks once her survival was confirmed.

If the initial shock and concern captured the world's attention, the positive spirit despite the loss of a limb by the cute, young, sun-kissed victim held it. Suddenly, the world had a poster girl for determination.

And it rejoiced in her triumph less than four weeks later when she took to the waves again, defying the odds by surfing again. As if that wasn't enough to serve notice to the surfing world that she wasn't fading away just because she'd lost an arm, Bethany stormed through the heats to claim fifth place in a National Scholastic Surfing Association meet while refusing any special allowances, only three months after her attack. Two months after that, she took fifth at the 2004 NSSA national championships. Her upward arc continued, and by summer 2005, she had claimed her first NSSA national championship at Salt Creek, California.

Bethany Hamilton is more than just a survivor. Her celebrity comes from more than mere novelty. She's been called the "surf miracle" by water mags. And she continues to prove time and again that she is still a surfer first—and one whose goals of one day winning a pro championship are not just a pipe dream.

Yet the most important part of Bethany's story is the divine element.

"God could have picked anybody, but He is using a teen surfer girl who gets her arm bitten off by a shark to be His spokeswoman to the world," Walking on Water director Bryan Jennings says. "He is speaking through her to this generation."

"Bethany's one of the most humble people on earth, yet she's one of the most known surfers of all time," filmmaker Nic McLean says.

From the start, Bethany has credited her faith in Christ as the source of her strength. Every chance she gets, Bethany keeps talking about Jesus in her soft-spoken yet straightforward way. She's become an international role model and celebrity of sorts, but she's still an ordinary teen girl—just one who understands that God uses ordinary people, teens included, to play important roles in His story.

HAWAIIAN HOME

I met up with Bethany and her mom, Cheri, on Kauai. Bethany is learning to ride her horse, Koko, and her instructor has her riding with no hands to improve her balance. Bethany is getting the hang of it, even when the young horse starts bucking. There's not much this girl won't try, with or without two arms.

The scene is typical Hawaiian: amazing. The red-dirt riding arena is set among lush green pastures sitting on bluffs overlooking the ocean. We walk to the edge of the 100-foot cliffs, where picture-perfect barrels are breaking on the beach below and whales are breaching offshore.

Here, the frenzied world of public appearances couldn't seem more distant. But Bethany has appeared on most major TV news shows, including "20/20," "Good Morning America," "The Early Show," "The Today Show," "Oprah" and "CNN Live." She's been featured in *Sports Illustrated*, *People*, *Life*, *ESPN*, *Outside*, *Surfer*, *Surfing*, *SG* and many other major magazines. She's been given awards like ESPN's 2004 Comeback Athlete of the Year and the U.S. Sports Academy Courage Award. Her autobiography, *Soul Surfer*, was released in October 2004 and made the *Los Angeles Times* Bestseller List. Her latest book, *Devotions of a Soul Surfer*, came out April 2006. A movie deal is also in the works. The girl's got her own fragrance line, Stoked for girls and Wired for guys, plus a line of jewelry and accessories at Claire's.

Kauai seems far from all these endeavors and opportunities. If there's an easy place to go with the flow, this is it. In fact, Cheri says living on the small, rural island helps keep life sane for her. Nevertheless, coming close to death, losing a limb and being barraged with media requests are no small trials, especially for a 15-year-old. The family receives about 20 requests a day for interviews, endorsements or appearances. "We turn down most of it 'cause Bethany has schoolwork to get done," Cheri says. "We'd have to shut down our life and travel all over, and she'd never get to surf again."

Bethany would rather focus on surfing, hanging out with friends, bringing encouragement to others and deepening her relationship with Jesus.

"One of the things I've learned comes from Jeremiah 29:11: ' "For I know the plans I have for you," declares the Lord, "plans to prosper you and not to harm you, plans to give you hope and a future," ' " Bethany says. "It tells me that God has a promise for my life and not to worry about it and try to go with the flow—even though I don't always."

SENSE OF ADVENTURE

The belief that God spared Bethany's life for a reason keeps her and her family going.

"I'll never forget this," says Troy Gall, Bethany's youth pastor at the North Shore Christian Church. "At the hospital the day after the attack, she told her brother Noah she was glad it happened to her so she could share Jesus with the world."

"You've got to do what God wants you to do," Cheri says. "That's where the adventure is, and our heart is to reach out into the secular world. All the interviews we do are so beyond us. We just pray, 'God, we can't do this. Please give Bethany something to say.' It's been really neat, because she says really cool stuff."

"I try not to make a big soap opera out of the shark attack," Bethany writes in *Soul Surfer*. "I would rather focus on what God has allowed me to do in picking up the pieces of my old life and adjusting to parts that are new and different for me. Most of all, I want to use my story as a way to tell people about God's story. It seems like He has given me the attention of the world for a moment and I had better take advantage of it while I can."[2]

That doesn't mean life is always easy. "My sister's still the same quiet person," says 23-year-old brother Noah. "She's not into the whole celebrity stuff, but God's given her an opportunity to be a witness for the world. I think at times she'd like to act like Jonah and run from God's plan."

Who could blame her? Many people would be crushed or consumed by such a horrific ordeal. Instead, Bethany has taken advantage of her opportunities to reach others. She has called other teens who've lost an arm. On a media tour of New York City, she gave her coat to a homeless girl and canceled a shopping spree she'd been given, saying she already had too much. She has visited amputees in military hospitals in Europe. She traveled to Asia to conduct tsunami relief through her partnership with World Vision, an international Christian relief organization. There, she encouraged children who had lost parents and loved ones, helping them to overcome their fears of the ocean by helping them to surf.

Bethany believes that it's all part of the mission she's been given. "I think God wants me to do this for Him, to care for people," she told the Associated Press following an announcement that she would promote Subway's "Be a Champion" program to encourage kids to eat healthy and be active.[3]

SICK SURFER

As if there were any questions remaining, Bethany has served notice that she's more than a novelty act. The girl is a serious surfer.

The NSSA national championship may have been her biggest victory of 2005, but earlier that year, she also dominated the O'Neill's Junior Pro Island in 4- to 6-foot surf on Kauai and earned invitations to the 2005 Vans Women's Triple Crown of Surfing on Oahu's North Shore. There, she charged double-overhead 12-footers in the 2005 Roxy Pro North Shore at Hale'iwa. And she was among the 7 wildcards invited to join the world's top 17 pros in the 2005 O'Neill World Cup of Surfing Women's Challenge at Sunset Beach.

"It's amazing to me that she can still go out there and compete and win and stay at that competitive level," says Keala Kennelly, a consistent Top 10 ASP pro and the leading female big-wave charger. "I couldn't do it. I really don't think I could do it."[4]

Bethany drew praise from *Surfing* magazine for her ability to belt out "I'm So Excited" in the dawn warm-up at Sunset as well as for her impressive surfing. Evan Slater described the scene: "Pancho Sullivan [who eventually won the men's Op Pro Hawaii] was out with her in the morning, giving her a few tips and showing her the lineup, when she swung around on a solid, 6-foot west peak and carved it to the channel. 'What she did at Hale'iwa blew me away,' said Pancho. 'But this is just a whole other level.'"[5]

"A lot of people don't really think I can surf, but I like to show them what I can do," Bethany told the Associated Press. "It definitely makes me known as a surfer."[6]

And all that with one arm. Have you ever tried paddling out using only one arm? Bethany has had to make a few minor modifications since the attack: adding a hand strap to the top center of her board that allows her to hold on while duck-diving under oncoming waves, and taking off later in bigger waves to compensate for lost paddling power.

But once in the water, you'd never know the goofyfooted girl is shorthanded. Watching her from shore carving up her preferred lefts, you can't even tell that her seaward left arm is missing. Her aggressive lines, cutbacks and floaters don't betray her.

As photographer for the U.S. Surf Team, A.J. Neste has spent time aiming his lenses at Bethany, who is a member of the team. He's continually amazed by her ability to maneuver so precisely in the water. "She's one of the best girl surfers out right now," he says. "I watch her, and I can't believe it. She's paddling with one arm, and then grabs that handle on her board and stands up and starts ripping."

Bethany's goal has always been to be a pro surfer. Despite her recent high-profile pro events, her plans are to stay off the tour full-time until she's 18. And she also entertains ideas of attending Bible college in Australia after completing high school. Whatever future path she follows, Bethany is already one of the most—if not *the* most—recognized female surfers in the world.

LIFE GOES ON

There's no doubt Bethany has grown and matured through her ordeal. But no matter how much fame or support she has, she still faces normal, everyday challenges.

"I've struggled with friends falling away from the Lord and doing dumb stuff that I can't understand," she says. "I was reading in the Bible where it says, 'Why do you look at the speck of sawdust in your brother's eye and pay no attention to the plank in your own eye?' [Luke 6:41]—basically, try not to judge your friends and ignore your own problems. I was getting all bothered with my friends, but there's stuff that I need to deal with in myself. I still need to care about them but look inside at myself."

Noah credits Bethany for her choices. "She's really wise about what she puts into her life and who she lets influence her. She really tries hard to be a leader," he says. "It's like the saying, 'Garbage in; garbage out.' She doesn't put any garbage in. She reads her Bible every day. Last year, she read the whole Bible."

That's a practice Bethany recommends to others going through tough times. "Read your Bible, and try to focus on the positive," she says. "And pray a lot. That helps."

THE SWELL ROLLS ON

Bethany's been through a lot. I never met her before the shark attack, but I'm struck with the sense that she probably wasn't much different then.

"Obviously, she has a better picture of God being her sustainer in every aspect of life and an understanding of His care," her youth pastor, Troy, says. "But Bethany has always been like she is now."

A.J. is impressed by her normalcy among her peers on the U.S. Team. "She's a normal kid, just having a good time," he says. "It's refreshing to see that. All the girls are hanging out, having a good time, laughing. It's amazing how much laughter comes out of these girls. Bethany's always right there in the middle of it. She's funny; she's a cut-up."

Basically, Bethany's simply a surfer girl God has chosen to use, and she'll keep riding whatever wave He sends. "I'm not perfect," she says. "I fall down and get back up. I just try and follow Jesus 'cause He's the ultimate role model. Jesus is my every day."

Waves of the World

You've gotta love it that the earth's surface is 70 percent water. If only you could guarantee that the swell was always headed your way.

The goal of the ASP world championship tour is to put the best surfers on the best waves around the world. The tour's schedule reads as a list of dream waves:

Gold Coast, Australia

Surfing is one of the most popular sports Down Under. Situated within the 300 miles of epic coast on the continent's eastern point, "the Goldie" spans about 50 particularly wave-wealthy miles and includes prime breaks such as Burleigh Heads, Snapper Rocks and Duranbah.

Bells Beach, Australia

Located on Oz's southern coast, Bells is way Down Under, about an hour southwest of Melbourne. The right-hand break has long been considered a classic.

Teahupo'o, Tahiti

Teahupo'o (pronounced Cho-poo) is the world's heaviest wave, due to the unrivaled thickness and volume that it churns onto shallow reef. It's the epitome of pure beauty when it's going off, but its hold-a-line-and-tube-ride-for-your-life is only for true masters.

Tavarua and Namotu, Fiji

The tiny Pacific island of Tavarua boasts two of the world's best lefts, Cloudbreak and Restaurants, which serve long and perfectly shaped barrels. Nearby Namotu offers more high-performance tubes.

Pacific Coast, Mexico

Our nearby southern neighbor has been a longtime favorite destination of California surf travelers. In the north, the Baja peninsula offers gems around the Cabo San Lucas area, and Todos Santos Island's monsters can reach 35 feet. On the mainland, Puerto Escondido is known as "the Mexican Pipeline."

Jeffrey's Bay, South Africa

Located at the southern coast on the Indian Ocean, J-Bay is the home of long, fast right points. It's an enormous bay filled with insane spots that include Boneyards, Impossibles and the center-piece: Supertubes.

Chiba, Japan

Japan is a nation composed of islands with thousands of miles of coast. Chiba lies off of the largest island, Honshu, and is one of the most popular breaks in the country.

Trestles, California

Located between San Diego and Orange County, Trestles has been described as the United States' most consistent wave. The state park-accessed breaks also stand out as an undeveloped oasis amid the highly developed SoCal coast. Lowers is the premiere break; Uppers and Church can also light up.

Southwest Coast, France
The 400 miles of southern Atlantic coast are home to Europe's oldest surf culture. Hossegor is often called the world's best beach break. Guethary and Lafitenia are stand-out reef breaks, as is Biarritz, the birthplace of European surfing.

Mundaka, Spain
Located in Spain's Basque region (north along the large Atlantic-facing Bay of Biscay), Mundaka is a fast and hollow left. When it's on, surfers can connect several tube rides for 300 yards.

Florianopolis, Brazil
Brazil boasts 5,000 miles of Atlantic coastline, and its southern region hosts the most consistent surf. The breach breaks Joaquina and Imbituba are some of the best.

Banzai Pipeline, Hawaii
Located on Oahu's North Shore, "Pipe" has long been considered the world's premier tube. Some big-wave riders devote their whole careers to mastering this monster, which is big enough to drive a bus through when it's going off. Although majestic, the reef break has proven deadly on occasions.

Types of Breaks

For many, surfing starts by getting pushed into whitewash off any old beach. But every surfer quickly learns there are vast differences in waves and the ways they break. Here's a primer.

Beach Break. Waves break on the sandy seabed. These are often the most gentle waves and are the best for beginners who are learning to surf. Hitting bottom is usually more forgiving.

Open-Ocean Wave. A wave that forms offshore along an underwater seamount. When conditions are right, the dramatic change in ocean topography can create a surfable wave as the water rolls up the underwater mountain and smacks into the peak. One of the best known locations for open-ocean waves is Cortes Banks, located about 100 miles off the coast of San Diego, where a 25-mile-long underwater mountain range rises from a depth of 5,000 feet to within 6 feet of the surface. Experts estimate this spot could create a 100- to 150-foot rideable wave.

Peak. A triangle-shaped wave (also called an A-frame) that forms a rideable face in both directions. One surfer can ride right and another left at the same time.

Point Break. A wave that strikes and then peels around a rocky point.

Reef Break. A wave that breaks over a coral reef or a rock seabed. Reef breaks are usually the classic, perfectly formed waves seen in photos and surf videos—but they can be rough on the wipeouts.

Rivermouth. Waves that form when a river meets the ocean and breaks over deposited sandbars or rocky ledges.

Slab. Technically, this is a reef break, but one with unique characteristics. A sudden, massive change of depth at the edge of the impact zone heaves up these unpredictable monsters. You can't even see this wave before it breaks.

Tidal Bore. These waves form in a small number of ocean-connected rivers such as the Severn in Britain, the Amazon in Brazil, and the Dordogne in France. The waves take shape when a higher-than-average tide funnels up a rivermouth into a narrowing inland passage.

Timmy Curran:
Higher Air

"I did my first aerial when I was 12," says Timmy Curran. "It was accidental. I was going down the line and had more speed than ever. I was just trying to go off the lip, but the backwash hit the wave right as I hit the lip so it threw me so high. It launched me way up in the air.

"I remember looking down and going, *Oh, my gosh, I'm in the air.* My feet were perfectly on the board. I was flyin', and I came down and ate it. I came up going, *That is the best feeling in surfing!*

"My family got it on video, and I remember slo-moing it and thinking I had something to do with it—which I totally didn't. But the feeling! I was completely captured by it. From then on I was trying airs on every wave.

"That lasted the next 20 years. I just kept going. You don't know how many waves I've completely blown going for airs, but that is why I surf. There is something about airs that I simply love."

THE AERIAL MASTER

Timmy Curran is an aerial master. His surfing has always been as much about performance above the wave as it is on it. It seems only fitting,

Vitals

Born: August 14, 1977

Home: Ventura, California

Family: wife, Shanoah

Sponsors: Hurley, Hoven, Adio, Channel Islands Surfboards, Famous Wax

Big Moment: First to land full flip (at least with documented proof)

More: www.timmycurran.net

then, that the trajectory of his career has followed the arcs of big boosts: a big blast upward followed by the inevitable drop. But part of being a big-air expert is being able to land the high-flying aerials, and Timmy has been able to absorb the shocks and gather more speed to continue relaunching to even greater heights.

The Oxnard, California, goofyfooter blew into widespread popularity as a 17-year-old when he opened Taylor Steele's 1995 adrenaline-charged video *Focus* by landing an aerial 360. His jaw-dropping performance played a big role in propelling Timmy to a Top 10 placement in the *Surfer* Poll awards at age 18, and he was the only non-World Championship Tour rider that year to be named as a Most Favorite Surfer. Quiksilver signed him up, paying six-figures for his promising talent. He was touted as the biggest threat to dethroning megachamp Kelly Slater.

The humble star seemed to take it all in stride, but the intense pressure took its toll and sent him into a tailspin. "Life is a ride of ups and downs, regardless of believing all your life in God," Timmy says.

At his low point, the 18-year-old phenom broke down following a poor contest showing and lost his motivation. For four months, he didn't even feel like surfing. Yet he rose from the foam, and by 1999 finished the World Championship Tour season at sixth place—only to drop off the Tour in 2000.

Of course, that didn't keep Timmy from continuing his aerial prowess and bringing in plenty of coverage for his sponsors. *Transworld Surf* magazine ranked him third for media exposure in 2002, and Timmy returned to the Tour in 2003. He enjoyed several years of moderate competitive success, and then chose to take some time off of the Tour after the 2005 season to devote more time to freesurfing, traveling and focusing on his music.

Through all the ups and downs, the aerial master has remained grounded spiritually and has spoken openly about his faith in Jesus. "Without Him, I wouldn't be here or have anything that I have now, so it's been fairly easy to speak about [my faith]," Timmy says. "I feel like I've had so many great opportunities to do that. I owe it all to Him, so it hasn't been too hard."

INTRODUCTIONS

Timmy Curran was born in Temecula, California, on August 14, 1977, and, like many of today's surfers, began as a 5-year-old with his dad pushing him into the whitewater at San Diego breaks. He was hooked from the start, and when his family moved to Ventura, he was a frothing grommet in the water at every opportunity.

It was the young boy's parents who introduced him to a relationship with God. As a 5-year-old, Timmy asked Jesus to live in his heart. "When you're that young, you're pretty pure and not as corrupted by the world," Timmy says. "So 'Jesus' and 'God' was a simple thing."

Growth and questions came as life rolled on. Timmy managed to dodge serious teenage rebellion or rejection of God, but he did experience a healthy process of figuring out what he believed and why. "When I was in my teens, I was like, *My parents believe it, but why do I believe it?*" Timmy says. "Once again, it was such a no-brainer to me. [My relationship with Christ] gives me a sense of purpose in this world. Without it, I'd feel like I was constantly searching for a purpose."

Timmy may fly like he's superhuman, but his spiritual life is a constant reminder to him that he's fully mortal. There's simply no way around that fact for anyone. It's not that we can't all follow God's plans and guidelines. It's just that we all will at times come up short of even our best intentions. "I'm constantly going against what God says. I'm constantly sinning," Timmy says. "I know I'm not supposed to, but that when I ask, I'm forgiven for what I've done. But I think in life and its day-to-day struggles, we're all idiots. We constantly rebel against God by our own choices. It's sad. I know I believe 110 percent about God and Jesus, but why do I still make these stupid decisions day after day?"

Comfort and the search for greater consistency come to Timmy through reading the Bible, attending church and maintaining accountability from his wife, Shanoah. "She is an amazing wife who is constantly seeking God, and she is a huge inspiration to me," Timmy says.

The pro tour can be a grind, keeping its members traveling on and off for 10 months of the year. That much time away from home can bring stress to anyone's life and relationships. For Timmy, it helps that Shanoah comes along nearly all of the time. "It is a grueling tour," Timmy says, "but I feel like the only thing you really miss is being able to tap into that church spiritual charge every

Sunday. I travel and hang out with the Hobgoods, and my wife travels with me 95 percent of the time, so I don't feel there is much of a difference."

And that's not all that keeps Timmy going. "Your Bible is everywhere. Reading and getting into the Bible—and obviously praying—are what give you that sense of God's peace," he says. "God is everywhere and His Word is everywhere, so it doesn't matter where you are."

NEW HORIZONS

When I mention Timmy's retirement from the World Championship Tour, he's quick to correct me.

"I never said I retired," he says. "I'm 28. I just decided to take a little time off."

Not time off from surfing, of course. He's just approaching it from a different angle. "I've always wanted just to do surf trips and not compete with anybody. Because of the industry, I'm able to have amazing sponsors who are just as pumped about my doing that as being on the Tour. I thought now is a good time just to go surf, have fun, make movies with Taylor Steele, work on some other little projects, and try a whole new way of doing the Tour without the Tour."

That means he'll still make a few contest appearances in between trips to super-spots like Tahiti and Costa Rica. But even those competitions will mean a welcome break from the highly competitive Tour. "Surf your brains out until you can't surf anymore—it's definitely less pressure," Timmy says. "I love it. I'm so thankful that I'm able to do this side of being a pro surfer."

As for those little projects, he can cross off the list becoming the first surfer to land an aerial flip. Photographer D.J. Struntz captured the insane acrobatic sequence at Oahu's Rocky Point for the April 2006 issue of *Surfing* magazine.

THE MAN AND HIS MUSIC

The way Timmy pushes the limits and explores the boundaries of wave riding are evidence of a creative side, so it should be no surprise that he has been devoting more energy to music. His six-song debut EP entitled *Citsuca* was released in April 2006 on Foe Records. It represented not only a labor of love a long time in the making, but also some answered prayers.

Timmy comes from a musical family, so it was natural for him to begin playing guitar when he was 13. His playing soon evolved into writing his own songs.

The first attempts of young musicians are usually a little rough, to say the least. Timmy says his were horrible, and apparently others agreed: "Even my girlfriend and family were like, *Oh, OK*. It was a little awkward for everyone. It felt like they were saying, *You're singing and making us feel uncomfortable.* I just played and played and always prayed, *God, give me a voice so I can sing in front of people without their getting embarrassed for me.*"

Persistence and prayer eventually came through—about 10 years later. The surf musician thought some of his songs were coming together a little better, and he finally got some positive feedback. "I played my wife one of my songs, and it was the first time that she was like, 'I like that song,'" Timmy says. "Then I played it to my brothers, and they were like, 'Whoa, Tim, we actually like that song.' It kind of went from there."

More songs. Live shows. The EP release with the potential of a full album in the works. The tune "Horses on the Range" was chosen for use in the soundtrack *Flow,* the 2005 film documenting the history of Al Merrick's Channel Islands Surfboards.

Stylistically, Timmy's sound is sparse and pure—a surfer and his acoustic guitar. Lyrically, it's questioning and introspective.

Timmy admits that creating music is a cathartic process. "I feel like the easiest songs for me to write are about things I'm struggling with or about people I care about who are going through tough times," he says. "I have the best life and job in the world, but we all go through crazy, heart-torn moments of sadness. Music is my release, and I'm able to get something off my chest when a song is done."

He probably won't be packing stadiums, but Timmy is happy that others can listen and connect with his songs. "It's been a wild ride, and I'm so thankful to God," he says. "I'm just enjoying the ride of the music venture. If it all ends today, I'll still be like, *Wow. It was way bigger than I ever thought.*"

You'd think a surfer like Timmy would be used to wild rides. Maybe he just holds on loosely, approaching life the way he does waves: charge for speed; hit it with all you've got; let it all fly and hope for a solid landing; whatever the outcome, remain thankful.

"If my whole career ended this second, I would have no regrets," Timmy says. "I would be so content and full. It was more than I ever dreamed of being able to see and do. The only thing I'd want to be remembered for is being a man who loved God and knew that God is responsible for everything. I am nothing without Him. That's the bottom line."

Deeper Than Appearances

It doesn't take a rocket scientist to realize that surfing is hot. Just look around the mall. Glance at school campuses. Check out advertising campaigns and media outlets.

Fashion can be a powerful influence, especially in youth culture, and a quick look at style reveals that surfing has become a driving force in mainstream culture. Malls across the Midwest are stocked with merchandise influenced by the surf lifestyle. Surf brands such as Quiksilver, Roxy, Hurley and Billabong are popular mainstays in large department stores and smaller chains, and young people living miles from an ocean seek out their styles and brand identities.

The lure of the surging ocean and sun-kissed beaches, the laid-back spirit of lounging in the sun, and the good-time vibe of hanging with friends draws consumers to the fresh, edgy styles of the surf fashion and board sports industry. Abercrombie and Fitch and American Eagle Outfitters make no apologies about paddling into the popularity of the surf culture, splashing life-size images of beach scenes on their walls and catalogs, and riding waves to greater profits. Even Paris, France, the fashion capital of the world, has been swayed by surfing's influence.

Surfing has clearly spilled over from its coastal birthplace, spreading into landlocked heartlands and far-flung foreign nations.

Shaper Eric Arakawa was surprised by the strong surf culture in Israel. "I was actually there for surfing business, of all things," he says. "I brought my family with me, and we stayed with a family on the coast in Herzliya. It's a beach community, but I couldn't believe how many surfers there were walking through the streets, on the beach, on the boardwalk, everywhere. If someone would have blindfolded me and asked 'Where are you?' I would have said the West Coast of California, maybe Huntington Beach. The kids were dressed in Billabong and Quiksilver. They looked like any kid in any surf town in the United States. It was an eye opener."

Where do you think the biggest *Noah's Arc* film premiere was? Los Angeles, California? Jacksonville, Florida? Nope. Boise, Idaho, a mere 20 hours from the coast, drew the largest crowd the film's creators have seen worldwide. Even a college class on surfing at Drew University in Missouri is regularly standing-room only.[1] Can you get any more heartland than that?

Pop culture has gone global, and surfing has found a place on the leading edge.

As the world becomes a more unified market, a global awareness and a sense of social responsibility are also flickering and spreading. Many corporations are trying to operate by a newfound conscience; some even give back profits to various causes. The environmentally driven One Percent for the Planet has proponents such as Patagonia.

Companies taking a stand allow consumers to buy quality products and services while at the same time putting their money toward something they believe in. The causes run deeper than profits, and corporate power is leveraged for good.

In this environment, several surf companies have chosen to operate by a spiritual conscience. Some are small. Some are large. Some are rising rapidly. Some may remain regional. But brands including Jedidiah, Cobian, Transformed and Not of This World are building their businesses on Christian principles.

Some use Scripture references or terminology in advertising or product creation. Some prefer to pick up subtler biblical themes. All promote a cleaner image and a quality product. Each aspires to a higher standard in ethical operations and calls on consumers to join in seeking more than what the temporary material world has to offer.

Will a T-shirt or pair of sandals change your life or make you a better follower of God? Probably not. But, can buying them from a company that chooses to avoid sleazy sexual advertising and images bring a shift to an often dark and perverted media culture? Possibly. Would digging deeper into the page of an ad or a phrase on a website to find the God of the universe revolutionize your soul? Definitely.

Jedidiah: Rooted in Love

Our company tag line, "rooted in love," comes from Ephesians 3:17. As a believer in Christ, I am blown away by how deep and wide the love of Christ is. Our goal with our brand is to inspire thought and questions that lead people to search their own hearts about who they were created to be. Our hope is that we start people on a path of seeking the truth about their lives and that on this journey they will find the loving God who is there waiting for us all.

No, a clothing company cannot change lives. But what a clothing company can do is promote an image, an alternative, a thought or an ideal. We want our brand to be a bridge or a connector to people with questions. We believe that everyone has a desire to belong to something. Jedidiah is trying to be part of a bigger community that desires to help less fortunate people. Through our friends at Invisible Children, World Vision, Glue and other places, we are trying to let people know that there is a network of like-minded people with a heart to serve others, rather than expecting life to serve them.

Jedidiah is connected to athletes, artists and musicians who don't yet know Christ. We feel this is a strong part of what God wants us to do on a daily basis: to show character and integrity to the people who have been put in our lives. We do not try to separate ourselves [as if we are] any better or above it all. We feel we need to be in the culture in order to make a difference. We obviously love the Christian community and deeply desire their support. But as a company, we are more invested in trying to reach outside this community [to] touch the hearts of the people who don't have a relationship with God. More at www.jedidiahusa.com

—Kevin Murray, Owner/President

Cobian: Walk with Us

"Some people have a business plan and financing. Cobian was a step of faith," says owner John Cobian about his company, which was founded with just $25,000.[2]

His is a David and Goliath story, as the company continues to grow side by side with such industry giants as Billabong and Quiksilver. The core values Cobian set from the start have served the company well. Today, they are creating some of the best footwear in the action-sport industry.

But on a deeper level, the company is founded on something more durable and resilient than materials and design. Cobian and his company stand firm on the words of 2 Corinthians 5:17, "Therefore, if anyone is in Christ, he is a new creation; old things have passed away; behold all things have become new." The company's tagline issues an ongoing invitation to all: "Walk with Us." (More at www.cobianusa.com).

Transformed: Death to Conformity

"We live in a culture that embraces choice, alternative modernity and perversion—a culture that exploits the weak and calls it ambition," says cofounder Jayson Payne. "It's a culture that preaches progress and yet is in need of reformation."

Transformed Clothing Company offers a new battle cry: "Death to Conformity. Renew your Mind." This battle cry and the company's name are based on Romans 12:2, which says, "Do not conform any longer to the pattern of this world, but be transformed by the renewing of your mind."

"We believe in innovation," Jason says. "We want to transcend socio-cultural barriers and the onslaught of perversion in contemporary fashion by selling clothing that defies the world's expectations." (More at www.transformedclothing.com).

Aaron Chang: Capturing Living Light

The empire was crumbling. The dizzying heights of success were becoming just plain dizzying as the harsh reality of failure came crashing down hard.

It was as if Aaron Chang was caught in the impact zone at Pipeline. The beautiful, mystical, picture-perfect wave can turn menacing and deadly in an instant. Pipe is a wave for experts, and Aaron Chang knew it well. He had surfed and photographed there for decades.

His expertise had also carried him to the top of the business world. What started with several T-shirts featuring his ocean scenes exploded into a hot apparel company. He had become a millionaire and was widely considered the best surf photographer around. In 1994, longtime *Surfer* and *The Surfer's Journal* photo editor Jeff Divine said of Aaron, "People always ask me who the best surf photographer is, and I've always said Aaron Chang."[1]

The devastating attacks of September 11, 2001, served as a wake-up call to many Americans. In the economic fallout that followed, the Aaron Chang company lost crucial funding. The bottom had dropped out, and the world of the millionaire was quickly spiraling out of control.

Vitals

Born: August 9, 1956

Home: San Diego, California

Family: wife, Erika, and son, Saxon Thomas

Team Riders: Will Tant, Carl Wallin, Adan Hernandez, Josh Vanderwaall, Tyler Reid, Sean Fowler

Big Moment: His photo of Mike Parsons riding a 65-foot wave at the Cortes Bank in January 2001 documented perhaps the biggest wave ever ridden.

More: www.aaronchanggallery.com

It was at the bottom that Aaron looked up and found help—and more—from God.

"It is a classic story of brokenness," Aaron says. "I was blinded by a very abundant life and quite a bit of success. In hindsight, I realize [that it's] the arrogance of human nature to deny God when everything is going well. My story is a classic story of God stripping that down and breaking me to a point where I realized the bigger truth."

ROOTS AQUATIC AND VISUAL

Aaron Kem Chang was born in Tucson, Arizona, on August 9, 1956. His parents were both school teachers, and they introduced their son to the ocean during summer vacations at San Diego's Pacific Beach. When Aaron was nine, his family moved to Imperial Beach, and the boy quickly progressed from riding an air mat to a longboard.

He also became an outstanding swimmer—so good, in fact, that he claimed a high school state championship in breaststroke during his junior year. At the time, this may have seemed the greater achievement, but eleventh grade was also the year in which Aaron took his first photography class to round out his course schedule.

When a broken ankle kept him out of the water, Aaron pointed a Super 8 video camera at his friends surfing near the Imperial Beach pier. The fun came in showing the footage to its "stars," and something sparked inside the creative teen.

Yet his dream had always been to surf Hawaii. So at 17, as soon as he graduated from high school, Aaron crossed the Pacific, found a place to live in a tool shed, and began surfing the fabled North Shore with newfound friends, such as Mark Foo and Bobby Owens.

The only problem was that Aaron's longtime friend and partner in Hawaiian dreaming, Mike Kraftson, was still on the mainland. "I started to take pictures to try and entice him to come over," Aaron says.

The endeavor turned into a job for a postcard company. Between this and peddling pictures of surfers to themselves during picturesque sessions, Aaron made enough money to eat—usually. Besides, even if he was hungry, he was surfing about 80 percent of the time. Life was great.

THE UNCORPORATE LADDER

In 1976, Aaron released a Super 8 surf movie called *Out of the Blue*, which he had filmed during the winter season on the North Shore. He returned to California to tour the project during the summer. Thinking a *Surfing* review would be helpful, Aaron stopped by the magazine's offices and ended up meeting photo editor Larry "Flame"

Moore, who encouraged Aaron to concentrate on still photography.

Aaron followed the advice, and when a staff photographer position opened at *Surfing* three years later, he jumped at the chance to be paid to travel the world shooting photos—and riding curls—in exotic locations.

Strong swimming skills and comfort in big waves gave the budding photographer confidence. There were few conditions he wouldn't go out in. The beautiful backdrops certainly played a role, but Aaron's artistic mastery propelled him to broad recognition even outside the surf world. High praise came from nonsurfing sources such as *American Photographer*, and his work appeared in publications ranging from *Sports Illustrated* to *Newsweek* to *Elle*.

"He was by then expert in all aspects of surf photography: action shots (taken from water or land), portraiture, candids, landscapes, and lifestyle," writes Matt Warshaw in *The Encyclopedia of Surfing*. "His composition was masterful; the color palette he worked from was broader than that of any of his surf-world peers."[2]

"He has photos of places firing," *Surfing* contributing photographer A.J. Neste says. "The photos he puts out are always *really* good waves. Witch's Rock, Blacks, Pipeline—it's always picture-perfect waves."

Once the surfing boom of the '80s hit, Aaron was poised to ride the wave to even greater success. He was clearly on top, and he demonstrated a shrewd business sense by capitalizing on his fame beyond the surfing realm, shooting high-paying and prestigious projects for companies such as Nike and Levi's.

By the mid-'90s, bootleggers had realized the value of selling T-shirts featuring images of Aaron's *Surfing* covers. Once the illegal copies were stopped, the photographer realized what a lucrative endeavor the pirates had discovered. Aaron's wife, Erika, put her degree in business and marketing to work and began the couple's own company selling clothing featuring Aaron's visual creations.

Photo Active Wear evolved into Aaron Chang Clothing. It seemed that Aaron had the Midas touch in business as well: In half a decade, Aaron Chang was a multimillion-dollar company. The empire was roaring.

TAKING IT ON THE HEAD

"Most people's lives from the outside look beautiful, until you get to the heart of when things are not right," Aaron says.

A photographer should know this. But all of us like to think that we're immune.

Aaron was no exception. After all, the self-described ambitious, passionate overachiever seemed to be shooting through the tube ride of a lifetime. Who could foresee that this wave wouldn't hold its size? The lip was about to come down hard.

The wake of 9/11 brought the closeout. The money came up short. The business was going down. A photographer feeds on light and clarity. Now there was only darkness.

Suddenly, everything in Aaron's life was churning: his work, his financial stability, even his family. The man who had once been dubbed *Qai Chang*, the quiet master, was now gripped by confusion, fear and panic attacks. "Everything was on the line," Aaron says.

It's a painful place for Aaron to revisit. He describes the period using terms such as "unbelievable," "painful," "stripped of defenses," "alone."

"It was the pendulum swing from my smug egocentric life to a point of realizing there are forces at work much bigger than myself here," he says. "It was not an easy process; it was very difficult. And to recover from it took a trinity [and more] of support. It took a good pastor and church. It took a good counselor. It took a good attorney—and one great God."

RESURFACING

In the midst of the chaos, a friend invited Aaron to church. There, another Christian read to him Ephesians 6:10-18:

> Finally, be strong in the Lord and in his mighty power. Put on the full armor of God so that you can take your stand against the devil's schemes. For our struggle is not against flesh and blood, but against the rulers, against the authorities, against the powers of this dark world and against the spiritual forces of evil in the heavenly realms. Therefore put on the full armor of God, so that when the day of evil comes, you may be able to stand your ground, and after you have done everything, to stand. Stand firm then, with the belt of truth buckled around your waist, with the breastplate of righteousness in place, and with your feet fitted with the readiness that comes from the gospel of peace. In addition to all this, take up the shield of faith, with which you can extinguish all the flaming arrows of the evil one. Take the helmet of salvation and the sword of the Spirit, which is the word of God. And pray in the Spirit on all occasions with all kinds of prayers and requests. With this in mind, be alert and always keep on praying for all the saints.

"That was the moment for me when the Word of God came alive," Aaron says. "That [Scripture] not only provided hope, but it also provided an awareness that God was waiting and right there. It was the lowest moment and the greatest moment in my life. In hindsight, all the pain and all the process and the suffering I would do again to get to that same point."

The road ahead was far from easy. It was, in fact, a painful process of healing. Aaron talks about those days with a sense of being rescued, a sense of being given back what he now realizes he really did not deserve. "God dismantled my life, which needed to be done," Aaron says. "I really dove into the Word and tried to rebuild my life on a different platform, a God-based platform."

Last-minute money came through to save the business from bankruptcy, although the resulting licensing agreement removed Aaron from direct control. A strange-sounding structure in a brand bearing his name, but it inadvertently allowed Aaron much more time to devote to rebuilding and strengthening his family and new-found faith. Aaron, Erika and their son are closer now than ever.

"We're bonded with each other through God in a way that I could never have imagined," Aaron says. "Basically, the apparel company is the mechanism that was at the root of all our calamity and disaster. It's also the mechanism that brought us to God."

INTO FOCUS

Throughout the ups and downs of Aaron's personal and professional worlds, photography remained a constant. Yet even the master's artistry has been revolutionized by his spiritual rebirth.

"I entered into photography purely to record the wonder that I had for the things I was seeing," Aaron says. "I used to tell people I would sense God when I entered the water to swim out into big surf. But I didn't really understand what I was saying; it just sounded cool."

Now Aaron is able to capture the visual wonders of creation in order to point people toward the Creator. "[God] transformed my work from a random collection to a more focused purpose," Aaron says. "I try to present things [in such a way as] to make people stop for a second and appreciate the immense beauty that we are surrounded with and the love that God is trying to reach us with. I really think I have something to say now."

The artist has also noted big changes in the artistic process. He has a new peace and a new patience. "I think a lot of creatives run on a fear-based process and this need to be loved and accepted," Aaron says. "It's interesting when you find you are loved and accepted and you don't need that from other people."

It was a strange realization for Aaron. He has replaced the old patterns of trying to manage and control the fears of what might go wrong on a shoot with a dialogue with God. Aaron believes it has led ultimately to better art.

"What has resulted is much better photography: much more truthful, much less contrived, much less trying and a lot more graceful [process]," he says. "I am trying to be in tune in a spiritual sense so that I can communicate through my work the beauty of this creation as best as I can interpret it."

Ever the visionary, Aaron has begun a new venture, Living Light Media, which seeks to provide new outlets for spiritually relevant print, video, film and live media projects to communicate Aaron's newfound "provocative and countercultural ideas." The company's first endeavor was a partnership with Christian Surfers International that resulted in *The Christian Surfers New Testament*, which featured Aaron's photography and testimonies of top surfers.

"It's all really still a new thing for me," Aaron says. "But it's amazing to me that if you harness what God has given you and you synchronize it with His effort, the results are, as Scripture tells us, more than you can imagine."

Man on a Mission

I would like to convey through photographs a sense of wonder with the amazing design or architecture of life. In the overwhelming perfection of the design is where I find God. It is my hope that when presented with the beauty and majesty of His creations, viewers might ponder the gift of life given to us so freely. It is our nature to become easily blinded to this beauty and to forget what a wonder it is to be alive. My hope would be that my photographs cause the viewers to appreciate what surrounds them and the joy of being alive.

—Aaron's Mission Statement
www.aaronchanggallery.com

The Motion of Pictures

Clichés become clichés for a reason: There's usually some truth behind them. Take, for example, "A picture's worth a thousand words." The ancient storytellers served their purpose, passing down important information, tales, truths and legends, but early man carved crude pictures on cave walls, trying his best to create visual wonders or to pass on helpful tips with a few strokes of a stick rather than a long list of words.

A skilled wordsmith can paint a moving verbal picture that can evoke strong emotion and stir passionate action. But sometimes words just don't do the job. A picture can trigger a landslide of feeling with one glance.

And that's just a still image. Add motion, music, effects and the senses are stirred. It's why our pop culture worships at the idol of Oscar. It's why Hollywood is one of the world's biggest power brokers. It's why the surf movie has been a mighty force in portraying and promoting the sport and lifestyle of surfing throughout its modern history.

If you can't be surfing, what's the next best thing to do? Watch others—who are probably better than you—rip choice waves.

Nic McLean, Director
Noah's Arc, Foundnation, Foundnation Project, Delbert's Metamorphosis

My dad was always encouraging me and my brothers and sisters to do creative things. Eventually, he handed me a 35-mm camera to start shooting still pictures. I grew up in Fredrick, Maryland, right outside Washington, D.C. I used to work at snowboard resorts and just loved skating and surfing in the summertime. Everywhere I went I had my camera with me, and I started taking a lot of portraits and action shots of my friends.

A couple years later, my dad brought home a video camera. It was pretty tricked out for the time. I got into the effects and read the whole manual. The photography I loved now came to life, and I could do so much more with action. My friends and I actually named the video camera "Smith" because I had it with me so much.

I was good in sports and did well in school and was very popular, but I still had a void—not some huge screaming thing that everyone could see, just something I could feel in my heart. I went to Young Life, and the guy was talking about who Jesus was. My ears perked up and my heart seemed to beat harder. After a weekend retreat that fall, I went up to my bedroom on a Sunday night, knelt beside my bed, and prayed for the Lord to come into my heart.

I got really serious about pursuing film and video once I left high school. I went to my first day of film school at University of Maryland, Baltimore County, and I knew exactly what I wanted to do. I soaked up every class. Everything I learned I still use to this day.

So I finished school, moved to the Outer Banks, and I got invited to Noah Snyder's house for a Bible study. I walked in and there was Matt Beacham, Jesse Hines, all of the guys from the eventual *Noah's Arc* film, and a bunch of other local surfers. I felt like I had finally found a group of guys who were like me. They totally embraced me. That night, Matt Beacham said, "Hey, why don't we make a Christian surf video together?" I said sure. The next day, we were on the beach shooting and, literally, that's all I've pursued to this day.

That's been the consensus answer for surfers since 1953, when 41-year-old school teacher Bud Browne premiered *Hawaiian Surfing Movies* to a full house at John Adams Junior High School in Santa Monica, California. Viewers paid a 65-cents admission fee.

The 45-minute film launched a revolution. Before that watershed showing, the communication lines of the surfing world were limited. No magazines yet existed to tell the stories and display full-color photos of surfing spots and exploits. News of a new maneuver or killer swell was spread only by word of mouth and rumor.

Browne's new creation changed all that, bringing surfers together to watch the sights and sounds of surfing and be inspired. He captured and conveyed a collective stoke. The experience was almost as important as the film being shown, and early surf-movie premieres were known for their raucous crowds who would hoot, cheer, boo and throw popcorn and drinks—not to mention an occasional projector, if a movie was especially bad.

THE RISE OF THE SURF MOVIE

Early surf movies united a culture, bringing surfers together to be inspired by the early icons and pioneers who were pushing the ever-shifting boundaries of a new way of life.

Browne immediately realized he'd stumbled upon something. The former lifeguard and Naval Chief Specialist in Athletics quit his teaching job after his first film's success and began creating and releasing one new movie each year. His early works generally cost about $5,000 to make. He barely broke even, but his new career kept him in and around the water. For Browne's, his surf-centric lifestyle was success enough.

Browne's work set the paradigm: one man with a camera filming in and out of the water, editing, splicing and scoring the surf flick. Once the creation was done, Browne would hammer up hand-made promotional flyers on telephone poles and surf shop walls to promote the film. When it came to screening, he would narrate his production from the projector room while telling the projectionist when to fade or raise the musical soundtrack's volume.

By 1957, others jumped into making surf movies. Their collective work of the late '50s created the general format that is still largely followed today: little or no plot, just surf-action montages set to music that are occasionally interspersed with a skit, interview or short nonsurfing detour. It didn't take Hollywood long to jump on the accelerating bandwagon. *Gidget* was a screaming commercial success for Columbia Studios in 1959, setting off a mainstream string of surf-related releases.

Although these films sent Americans clamoring for the surf and seashores, Hollywood's surfers were highly stereotyped and generalized. Despite surfing's newfound popularity, its image was taking a beating at large. Most of the coverage in the early '60s from major mainstream press outlets such as *Time* magazine depicted surfers as drug-using, drop-out beach bums.

It was against this backdrop that Bruce Brown (no relation to Bud) released surf movies' greatest masterpiece: *Endless Summer.* Some of Brown's earlier releases, such as his 1958 debut *Slippery When Wet,* are considered classics, but *Endless Summer* became a landmark inside and outside the surfing subculture.

The 91-minute project followed two surfers traveling the world in search of the perfect wave. Like any other surf film, it premiered for surfers, but when it sold out seven nights straight in Santa Monica, Brown realized he had something special. He enlisted commercial help, converted his 16-millimeter format to 35-millimeter, and released *Endless Summer* at mainstream box offices, beginning with Wichita, Kansas, on a snowy 2° F night. It was a smash hit and proved to be so all across the nation, even receiving critical acclaim from media such as *Newsweek* and the *New York Times.*

The movie single-handedly turned the tide of public perception about surfing, elevating its status to a noble pursuit and enlightening the general public to the stoke of riding waves.

THE FORMULA

Despite the beauty and success of *Endless Summer,* the body of surf flicks is considered artistically mediocre. That's not to say these films haven't inspired countless surfers and nonsurfers, just that most of the nearly 300 titles released from 1953 to 1990 remained largely formulaic.

"Energy, not artistry, was the hallmark of the surf movie," writes former *Surfer* magazine editor and surf historian Matt Warshaw in the introduction to his book *Surf Movie Tonite! Surf Movie Poster Art 1957-2005.*[1]

Some standouts and classics include *Cat on a Hot Foam Board* (1959), *Surfing Hollow Days* (1961), *Waves of Change* (1970), *Morning of the Earth* (1972), *Free Ride* (1977), the Hollywood cult hit *Big Wednesday* (1978), *Storm Riders* (1982) and *Surfer: The Movie* (1990).

Surf movies fit nicely into the '80s era of music videos. In 1984, *The Performers* became the first surf film to release on video-cassette. The shift was on. VHS and DVD became the primary format, and collective viewings for surf movies trailed off. The genre lost is communal spirit and also suffered when music companies cracked down on bootlegged soundtracks in the early '90s.

ENTER THE CHRISTIAN RIPPERS

Christian surf movies date back to 1975, when the evangelistic *Tales from the Tube* toured surf theaters, promoted as "a Spectacular Surf Odyssey." But timewise, spiritual projects were fairly scattered.

The next Christian surf movie, *Shout for Joy,* came in 1983 and dramatized the life story and testimony of surf champion Rick Irons. (Rick, who is the uncle of top surf pros Andy and Bruce Irons, is now a pastor in Hawaii.)

Son Riders (1988) captured the spiritual surfing scene of the day, featuring action clips and testimonies of surfers such as Joey Buran and Mike Lambresi. *A Wave of Life* followed in 1990. Joey and Mike, among others, used the pair of videos for some fruitful outreach events.

Walking on Water Ministries, founded by Bryan Jennings, decided to get involved in the video genre by releasing *Follow the Leader* in 1998 in conjunction with All Aboard Films and Skate Street Ventures. The project included impressive surf footage of Tom Curren, C.T. Taylor, Joe Curren and Bryan Jennings, though some of the film had a somewhat homemade grain to it. That same year, *Beyond the Break* released Down Under.

Changes, released in 2000, represented a leap forward. The video combined sick clips of Tim Curran, Tom Curren and C.T. Taylor with stories of each surfer's encounter with God. There were poignant interviews with John Carper and Skip Frye, as well as a dramatic presentation of the story of the late Chris O'Rourke.

Technology was improving. Production was improving. The Walking on Water staff and video partners were gaining valuable experience. *The Outsiders* (2002) took a big step into full professionalism under the direction of Jesse Schluntz. The cast was first rate, including C.J. Hobgood (fresh off his 2001 world championship), Damien Hobgood, Tim Curran, Jesse Hines, Matt Beacham, Noah Snyder, and more. The footage was mind-blowing. The editing was clean. The storytelling conveyed the message of the gospel clearly and artistically. *Surfer* magazine ran an eight-page spread on the film, and *Transworld Surf* named it one of the best releases of the year.

The early millennium saw a larger return to the collective showing and viewing of surf films. The Walking on Water crew got on board and tried their hands at premiering *The Outsiders* in churches, theaters and community centers, even taking *The Outsiders* abroad to Japan.

Noah's Arc rolled out in 2004 and maintained the level of top-notch quality achieved by *The Outsiders*. This time, East Coast director Nic McLean was at the helm, documenting the spiritual journey of his friend Noah Snyder and incorporating rad action footage of the Hobgoods, Will Tant, Matt Beacham, Jesse Hines, and others. The result was a visually beautiful and moving documentary.

Walking on Water stepped up its touring efforts, taking *Noah's Arc* up and down the coasts of the United States, Japan, Europe,

Australia, South Africa and Central and South America. More than 85,000 people came to the premieres. Thousands responded to subsequent invitations to offer their lives to Christ.

Others found their own way to the DVDs, but ultimately found their way to God. "I ran into a kid at the Christian Surfers national conference," Bryan Jennings says. "I asked him, 'Why did you become a Christian?' He said, 'I was stoned one day in my house, and I watched *The Outsiders* movie. As I was watching, I got saved. For the last six months, I've been clean and sober and involved with Christian Surfers.' I was looking at him like, *Are you serious?!*"

Surf movies with spiritual themes make sense to director Nic McLean. "There is an innate void in each one of us," he says. "We all want to listen to a story that we can relate to and see ourselves in. Three hundred years ago, we watched theater. There was no option to have film. Even before that, in other cultures, stories told around campfires captivated hearts. I think the Spirit of the Lord is ready to move on people's hearts, because they're seeking something real. We're just making a way for people to receive the message."

Jesse Schluntz, Director

The Outsiders, Western Promise, Teardevils trilogy

Making surf movies is incredibly hard to do in an original way because it seems like everything's been done. There are so many cookie-cutter movies out there. They're all typical: punk rock music and a section of one guy's clips. Here's his name; here's him surfing. Next guy, next guy, next guy.

The biggest challenge to me is shooting video in a creative way. That means actually utilizing cinematography in a video format: the angles, the feel, the words, the audio. The challenge is finding different music, different angles, and editing with a clean style that varies a lot so you're getting deep. That's the coolest thing from a movie-making standpoint.

If you want to get into film, you first need mentors who know what they are doing. Second, you need to make projects. Make a little movie, and then get opinions. To be honest, it takes years. You have to work your way into getting on tours and shooting footage of surfers who are on the sidelines but who might become some of the best in the world. You've got to be prepared to sacrifice and really put your heart, soul, blood, sweat and tears into it.

But the pluses outweigh the minuses. I used to make all these movies for myself and live for the premiere night. All I wanted to do was get people stoked. Now as a Christian, I'm able to see people who are getting the gospel and getting stoked. We get people in a theater who would never go to church, and they hear the whole gospel. It's beautiful.

Bryan Jennings: At the Heart of Surfing

That's it! This Valentine's Day was bad enough with no girl to hang out with. Now it's getting downright catastrophic, God! You can't be serious.

I want you to give up surfing contests.

I'm outta here.

Get back in the chapel, Bryan.

Okay. Okay. I'm back in, but You can't be serious, God! I just lost and had a good attitude about it. There must be some kind of mistake. My surfing career is on the upswing, and giving up contests is not gonna help. I mean, You've got to be realistic about it. Come on, Lord, why are You going to make me do this?

I'm serious, Bryan. Trust Me.

All right, Lord. If this is really You, then I need a sign. When I walk out of this chapel, I need to see two people. Hmm . . . Melissa and Zoe. I haven't seen either one of them forever. Melissa and Zoe. If they're not out there, then I'll know this is just some crazy mind game.

Bryan Jennings walked out of the prayer chapel onto the beautifully manicured oceanfront campus of Point Loma Nazarene University in San Diego. Much to his relief, the campus looked pretty much deserted—except, *Oh no!*

Vitals

Born: May 17, 1974

Home: San Diego, California

Sponsors: Jedidiah, Cobian

Big Moment: First Walking on Water surf camp, summer 1995

More: www.walkingonwater.org

"Hi, Bryan."

"What's up, Bryan?"

Bryan could not believe his eyes: *Melissa and Zoe!*

"Oh, you wouldn't believe it," he said. *Whoa. Okay, God. But maybe they just happened to be walking by. This is insane, but I'd better get to my RA interview.*

"Bryan," the interviewer said, "We think you'd make a great leader and role model for other students as a resident assistant, but we've got one concern: your surfing contests. They seem to take up a lot of time."

Oh, man! Here we go again. This is crazy.

"Well . . . would you believe it if I told you that God just told me to give up the contests for a year? I'm still kind of trippin' on it, but that's where I'm at."

And that's where Bryan stayed: He gave up competitive surfing for a year. Not that he set aside the ocean completely, but the aspiring pro took a much more mellow approach, dropping out in a sense and riding only a longboard. Some might even say he returned to the purer soul of surfing. Bryan claims it actually improved his waveriding.

"The minute the year was over, I sent a fax to a bunch of surf companies, and Gordon and Smith Surfboards ended up sponsoring me," Bryan says. "That's when my pro surfing started officially. I got a lot of exposure through G & S, and they paid me a salary and supported me."

It may not have seemed as significant at the time, but Bryan's decision to follow God's path was a glimpse of what was to come. The young surfer set himself on a track of obedience, choosing to place God before surfing and to organize his life priorities spiritually. It was the first step toward a pattern that would come to mark the surfer's life and career.

CENTERED

If you begin connecting the dots of the bigger picture of God's work in surfing, you quickly realize that Bryan Jennings is as central a figure as there is. As founder and director of Walking on Water Ministries, Bryan is a man with a mission, but the mission is far greater than any one man—and he knows this. Bryan is a leader, a connector, a partner, an encourager and a motivator. Yet at the heart of it all, he is a surfer who cares most about serving his Creator and who wants to see others encounter Jesus.

"The move of the Holy Spirit and work of God in the surf industry should historically be linked with Bryan Jennings," says former top surf pro turned pastor Joey Buran. "What he has done with his movies and Walking on Water is absolutely unbelievable. He has been so effective and fruitful. Bryan is like the apostle to the surf community."

By giving up any selfishly motivated ambitions of a surf career, Bryan has been given back a surfing life that includes surf camps, surf movies, surf sponsorships and worldwide surf outreaches.

All of it he holds loosely, inviting others to replicate or participate.

"I want to see Walking on Water duplicated," Bryan says. "I want to see other people making surf movies, and I want to see other people doing Christian surf camps. I don't want to hold on to this vision and be like, 'No one else do it!' I want everybody to go do it. If we can do it, you can do it."

That open spirit plays out not only in the direction of Bryan's endeavors but also in their execution as well.

Mike Doyle, the director of outreach for Walking on Water since 2004, says he admires his boss's heart for the gospel, for people and for giving. "The thing I respect most is Bryan's openness to the Spirit of God," he says. "Working for him, he gives me almost complete freedom to follow after the direction I feel like God is leading."

"Bryan is a spokesperson for the young generation of surfers who have a relationship with Jesus," says Nic McLean, a film producer who has collaborated with Bryan, most notably on *Noah's Arc*. "He's also an evangelist. He's a guy who has a vision to see young people connect with Jesus."

BEGINNINGS

Bryan Scott Jennings was born in La Jolla, California, on May 17, 1974, and began surfing at age 10. The innocence of his childhood took a blow a year later when his parents divorced.

The family had never been religious. They attended church on average once a year for a seasonal service. But as the boy grappled with the fallout of his parents' split, he asked his mom what to do when he felt alone. Her answer was, "Jesus is always there with you." The concept planted a spiritual seed, though formal spiritual guidance remained nonexistent.

As a 14-year-old, Bryan was taken on the trip of a lifetime. Pro surfer Peter King took him to Hawaii for the first time. The wave riders paid homage to surfing's origins on Maui and Oahu's North Shore, and Peter took the opportunity to talk with the grom about spiritual matters. "He started telling me about the Lord and angels and demons and spiritual things," Bryan says. "I hadn't really thought about it much before. That really impacted me."

Another seed had been planted.

But as is often the case, the immediacy of adolescence trumped more eternal matters. By the time he was an 18-year-old student at La Jolla High School, Bryan was heavily into the party scene. "I was a little surfer kid trying to be fulfilled through what the world was telling me was fulfilling: popularity or a pretty girlfriend or drinking or being at the party," Bryan says.

The problem was, it didn't work. "It always made me empty. I would end up coming home [from a party] totally sad," Bryan says. "I remember crying myself to sleep a bunch of times, thinking, *What's my problem?*"

On one such night, the 18-year-old opened a Bible in his bedroom to Isaiah 1:18-20: "'Come now, let us reason together,' says the LORD. 'Though your sins are like scarlet, they shall be as white as snow; though they are red as crimson, they shall be like wool. If you are willing and obedient, you will eat the best from the land; but if you resist and rebel, you will be devoured by the sword.' For the mouth of the LORD has spoken."

"It really hit me: Which way do I want to live my life?" says Bryan. "Do I want to be willing and obedient? Do I want to live for the Lord? Or do I want to continue to rebel? I finally had had enough. I gave my heart to the Lord."

What took off immediately was Bryan's surfing. Admittedly, he had never done well in any big contests, but the Saturday after his spiritual surrender, he won a local pro-am contest.

At the encouragement of a friend, Bryan drove the next day to Huntington Beach to enter—and win—the bigger West Coast Pro-Am contest. He also picked up a Rip Curl sponsorship in the process, having asked the sales rep for one beforehand if he won.

The success was exciting for Bryan, but it also raised questions about what was going on in his life. "As I drove back that day, my pride was kind of angry at God because I knew I didn't win those contests," Bryan says. "It was like I was cheating. God gave me the perfect waves. Then another part of me was like, *Why are You blessing me, God? I've been a jerk for 18 years. Why are You blessing me a week after I became a Christian? Shouldn't I have to be punished for 18 years?* I didn't know what grace meant. I didn't know what His mercy meant."

The questions led the new believer to Romans 2:4: "Or do you show contempt for the riches of his kindness, tolerance and patience, not realizing that God's kindness leads you toward repentance?"

"It's like, *You are so good to me that I want to stop doing the wrong things,*" Bryan says. "I wish I could say at that point I stopped doing all the wrong things, but I didn't. For that next year I struggled."

But the journey had begun. Another surfer had surrendered to the Maker of the waves.

GOING CAMPING

Ten kids showed up in 1995 for the first Walking on Water surf camp.

"I just wanted to reach out to people and tell them about the Lord," Bryan says, describing his motivation. "I didn't have a plan to start a ministry. It was just the next step that God had given me in my heart."

But the idea gained momentum. Bryan pursued a competitive surfing career, and during the summers he taught kids to surf and to pursue Jesus.

The camp scene is typical: come for a week, stay in college dorms, spend the day honing surfing skills at La Jolla Shores or another beginner-friendly San Diego beach break, play pranks on friends and counselors, gather for devotional discussions and worshipful sing-alongs.

Bryan was initially surprised to find that most of the campers came from Christian families and church backgrounds. Not that he minded; these kids and teens need guidance as much as any. "They're struggling big time and have a lot of questions," he says. "It might be they're just not listening to their parents or youth pastors, but they are not getting those questions answered. It's awesome, because they come here and God allows us to answer those questions for them. They go away like whole other people."

Working with kids can be challenging, but it's also satisfying. "The first day is always fun, watching them get up in the water for the first time. They just love it," Bryan says. "And the last night, just hearing kids' hearts [when they share what they've learned]."

Bryan's surf career with a side of ministry was a good blend for five years, but eventually something had to give. Much travel and dedication are required to make it as a pro; much commitment and effort are necessary to host several hundred grommets each summer.

"Pro surfing was going pretty good, and Walking on Water was going pretty good, but neither was as good as it could be," Bryan says. "And they were both growing. I had to pick one or the other."

The choice was fairly easy, but it did mean that Bryan had to give up any visions of glory in order to give to others.

"Bryan has had a calling on his life," Nic McLean says. "I think that what he walked away from was the opportunity to seek self. I think that was a response to him listening to the call of his heart."

ROLL 'EM

Why not make a movie that glorifies Christ? Gather some friends, film some rad surfing, and talk about God? Bryan had thought for years about making surf films with a Christian message.

Follow the Leader was the first Walking on Water video. It released in 1998 and met with positive response. Surfers up and down the coasts realized that they were not alone in their faith. Kids across the heartland saw amazing surf footage and heard the message of God's love. Even *Surfer* magazine ran a feature story related to the project.

"I learned a lot about faith," Bryan says of the first project. "You gotta take that step of faith."

Outreach premieres also began with several Southern California showings, setting the pattern for Walking on Water's ministry to come. With practice came improvement, and *The Outsiders* and *Noah's Arc* stepped up the filmmaking professionalism.

"There is so much shoddy workmanship in the name of Jesus, and it really upsets me," surfboard shaper John Carper says. "But Bryan doesn't just slap together a bunch of guys surfing, throw a bunch of Christian music in it, and think it's good enough. Shane Dorian watched *The Outsiders* twice in a row [and told me] it was one of the best quality surf videos he's ever seen."

As Bryan and company began getting word out about their films, chapters of Christian Surfers International partnered with them, coordinating and hosting outreaches around the world. The events had a unifying effect among spiritually minded surfers, bringing them together in fellowship and ministry.

"Though there's always been a witness and Christian influence in surfing since the '70s, there has never been a combination of the quality films, outreaches and world evangelism that Bryan has done," Joey Buran says. "He's showcasing the quantity and quality of surfers representing Jesus Christ and the quantity of strong Christian influence in the industry. You've never had that combination like right now. Bryan has just nailed it with the gifts God has given him."

"For the last 10 years, Walking on Water has been growing, and Christian Surfers has been growing, too," Bryan says. "God's been doing this really neat thing in the Body of Christ. We all individually were following what God put in our hearts, and as we did, God blessed [our efforts]. It all added up to this amazing end result of a bunch of people coming to know the Lord and a bunch of believers being encouraged."

DREAM TRIPS

Now it's all come full circle.

A concept that's been brewing in Bryan's heart since the beginning is being brought to fruition as this book is being released. The idea grew from Bryan's own early-teen Hawaiian trip with Peter King: take two groms on the trip of a lifetime, ride world-class waves, encounter exotic cultures, connect with pro surfers, and serve those in unimaginable poverty.

"This is the one that I really wanted to make the whole time," Bryan says.

Tyler Hallen, 15, of Laguna Hills, California, and Luke Davis, 13, of Capistrano Beach are stoked that Bryan's dream is becoming a reality. As the featured groms, the two young shredders traveled to Hawaii, Peru, Australia, Indonesia, South Africa and Israel. The world truly became their classroom.

"God's helped me to just be thankful for all the things I have and to not take anything for granted," says Luke.

"It's pretty heavy that God chose me. There is a whole world of kids He could have picked," Tyler says. "But God must have taken me for a reason. I hope His reason is to get people to know Him."

The project also represents a completion of sorts for Bryan. As a primary personality in the movie, he is also surfing onscreen once again, proving that he still rips.

All of his Walking on Water surfing-related endeavors have drawn the attention and support of sponsors. "Jedidiah and Cobian are both sponsoring me," Bryan says. "They pay me, and it's like, *Whoa, I guess I am a pro surfer again.*"

His role aside, Bryan has high hopes for his latest movie. "My hope and prayer is that this film will be part of launching a revival," he says. "That's a pretty huge thing to say, but that's actually what I hope and what I think is realistic with God's strength and with God's abilities. If it is something that He wants to do, it will happen."

You've just got to take that step of faith.

"Walking on Water could end tomorrow. It could end up changing the whole world," Bryan says. "I don't know what the Lord wants to do. I just want to be willing and keep going to Him and asking what the next steps are."

Scene of the Scenes

One of my favorite premieres was in Dublin during *Noah's Arc* 2005 European tour at the largest skate park in the Republic of Ireland. It's this huge skate park by the airport in Dublin called Ramp City. It was just insane. We did a skateboard demo with the Apostle skate team that was completely packed with Irish kids, probably 300 to 400. We showed the film next, and Matt Beacham shared after the film. The guys who run the park said it was the best event they'd ever had there, better than all these events by pro-skate companies. The owner of the park, who wasn't even a Christian, absolutely loved it.

Another was in El Salvador, in a rough little beach town called La Libertad. Our point guy there was Salvador Castellanos, who is a CNN correspondent for Central America. He knew all the right people. We blocked off an entire city street, put up our projector, and showed *Noah's Arc* with Spanish subtitles in downtown La Libertad, surrounded by 20 members of an elite paramilitary security force, complete with machine guns. Salvador got up afterward and preached the gospel to the crowd, and about 60 or 70 people got saved. We passed out about 100 New Testaments and about 500 tracts, and God's Spirit moved. It was packed. It was awesome to see God move in El Salvador.

—Mike Doyle
Walking on Water Director of Outreach

Whose Wave Is It?

CHAPTER 16

What are you gonna do? Your favorite break is going off. You've checked the surf cams. The Pacific typhoons are pumping a perfect winter swell right up your beach break. The offshore winds are just right, setting up set after set of glassy barrels. Ah, liquid perfection.

It's your pipe dream come true—and your worst nightmare.

As soon as you get within a half mile of the paddle out, reality hits hard: cars line every inch of available curb with board racks empty; parking lots are packed. Cresting the final hill, the bittersweet scene sprawls across the horizon: azure corduroy flecked with the dark blotches of wetsuited demons.

The sea is packed. Everyone and his brother—heck, his sister too—is in the water trying to get a piece of this classic day. It's the most hectic lineup you've ever seen. You can almost hear the angry seagull-like chorus rising: "Mine! Mine! Mine!"

Your stoke takes a serious hit, but what can you do? Perfection is calling. You have to paddle out. *Maybe it's not so bad,* you reason to yourself, holding on to some illogical ripple of hope.

But once in the water, there's no way around the impact zone of the truth, and it comes heaving down hard, drilling you square on the head. The electric vibe of aggression skips across the surface like a lightning strike. Tempers flare fast and furious.

Riding Switch

What should a Christian look like in the lineup? Take it from some guys who've been in a few and know what it takes.

Damien Hobgood

The life of a surfer is kind of selfish in a way. It's something I look at a lot. You want to go to that spot and be the only one out or riding the best waves. You don't want anyone else to experience it. But that's contrary to what I believe. I have to think, *Look how awesome this wave is and look how many people are getting to enjoy this, and I'm going to get to enjoy it with them.* For sure, I've screamed at people in the water. I don't do it very often, but usually right after I say it, I think about how lame it was that I did that. There's always another way to resolve the problem.[1]

Skip Frye

The word *aloha* can be used in spiritual terms. It's love and sharing and all of that. The more you do that, the better the session is going to be. You get the good vibe going on. I've seen bad vibes get so bad that the ocean just stops, almost like it's saying, "Okay, you guys want to just sit here for a while and think about it?" It's like in Scripture when it says to let them see your good works or good life so that they may see God and glorify Him. Other surfers will go, "Hey, God is good. Who's this guy?" And they can relate you to God. A lot of people in my realm can because they know where I'm at with God."

Kahana Kalama

In surfing, it's easy to paddle out and reduce others as mere obstacles to me catching waves. It's easy to get competitive, calling or waving people off to get as many waves as possible. But understanding what it means to be rooted in love brings a new purpose to surfing. A lot of times surfing glorifies tough guys, and kids think they have to be tough. But it's about building relationships. Now I try to talk to and love on people in the water. Realizing that we're all broken, sinful and in desperate need of Jesus gives us common ground. Our only value comes from being loved by God.

Maybe one sick ride will ease the negativity that's bringing you down. And as the next swell begins to stand up, you're in the perfect position. Stroking hard toward shore, you know this is a gift from above. One more stroke. One fluid motion. One quick rise and you're dropping, dropping down the overhead beauty—suddenly, an obnoxious grom is above you, on you, dropping in late on your wave, cutting you off, sending you bailing into a ragdolled trip through the spin cycle.

By the time you wash up inside, your rage is, well, raging. All of your frustration is ready to fire and you can't wait to drill the kid who cut you off. He has got to pay.

Your paddling takes on a jet-fueled propulsion as visions of ripping his head off spur you on. You spot him in the lineup, laughing with his bros. He is gonna pay!

But duck diving through the break, your visions of vengeance are suddenly interrupted. *Love your enemies and pray for those who persecute you.*

What?! No! You are so in the right, and this jerk needs to pay!

Sure, you read that verse in your Bible study group. You even prayed about showing Christ's love in the lineup and on the shore—but come on, that was before the biggest snake of the year. God would understand, right?

Love your enemies and pray for those who persecute you.

You're coming in closer, and the jerk is still sitting in the lineup. He hasn't even seen you. Twenty more yards and you can blindside him with a right cross.

Arrgh. That verse. This conflict inside is raging even bigger than the one you want to start—and finish—with this kook.

What are you gonna do? What should you do? What does it mean to be a Christian in the lineup? It's a lot easier to talk about love and forgiveness from the safety of the shore than live them out in the water.

THE GOLDEN RULE

To get good waves, you've got to give a little and realize that the tides don't revolve around you. Most surfers (at their best, anyway) recognize and adhere to an unwritten code that honors a cooperative giving spirit. Perhaps Jesus captured the spirit best thousands of years ago when He said, "So in everything, do to others what you would have them do to you" (Matt. 7:12).

How hard is that? Treat others in and out of the water like you want to be treated. Sometimes it's way hard.

Being like Jesus doesn't mean you have to, or should, sit back while one kook makes the water unsafe and unenjoyable for everyone else. Jesus actually laid out some healthy steps for resolving conflict, and they apply to any situation, even the lineup.

Here's the way Jesus said it: "If your brother sins against you, go and show him his fault, just between the two of you. If he listens to you, you have won your brother over. But if he will not listen, take one or two others along, so that every matter may be established by the testimony of two or three witnesses. If he refuses to listen to them, tell it to the church; and if he refuses to listen even to the church, treat him as you would a pagan or a tax collector" (Matt. 18:15-17).

Not everyone who drops in on you will be your Christian brother, but he or she is a part of the greater community of the lineup.

Sometimes simply addressing another surfer personally may be enough to solve a problem. Sometimes the collective lineup might have to get involved to confront a consistently dangerous surfer. Either way, being like Jesus means keeping love at the core, unafraid to speak the truth and ready to extend forgiveness.

It also means remembering the bigger picture. Sometimes, that means giving up your own rights to fairness, justice and even good waves. Even more than whose wave is whose, God cares about how you respond, your attitude, how you view and deal with another human, how you learn from it—and, ultimately, how well you represent Him in the process.

Good Etiquette

Every decent surfer knows that a code of respect and safety must be followed. The ocean can be dangerous, and there's enough dynamic energy charging around the lineup without the addition of human stupidity.

Some of the rules are spoken, some unspoken. They aren't hard and fast. You can find different versions and sources. But here are 10 agreed-on basics for how to act and treat others in the water.

1. Choose Wisely

Pick a break that fits your ability and comfort zone. Whether you're a beginner or advanced, surfing a spot that doesn't fit can cause discomfort for you and others. Some spots are beginner-friendly and some are for masters. Be realistic.

2. Don't Rush In

This is especially important when surfing in an unfamiliar area. But even if you've ridden a break a million times, it's a good idea to scope things out before jumping in. Check the wave conditions, the weather and the crowd. You'll make better decisions in the water if you allow yourself a quick overview on land.

3. Follow Wave Priority Rules

Never catch a wave once another surfer has claimed it by being in a better position for takeoff. There are lots of ethics specific to avoiding cutting off and snaking. But basically, the rider closest to the wave has priority. If you drop in on accident, apologize and get off the wave quickly.

4. Take Turns

You've heard it since kindergarten: share. But by nature, we don't like to. However, with the popularity of surfing, it's not an option. When the line forms, take your place and wait your turn. And remember, it's your responsibility to be in a good position to catch a wave.

5. Stay Out of the Way

When paddling out, stay out of the area where waves are breaking and being ridden. It's easier to paddle, and you'll allow others a good ride. Always keep your board close and under control as much as possible to avoid injuring yourself and others.

6. Show Respect

Always respect other people, especially locals when traveling. A good vibe goes a long way in keeping it fun for everyone.

7. Protect the Environment

Use public restrooms whenever possible. Use trashcans, or take your trash with you. Tread lightly on nature. Leave the area better than when you arrived, ready for the enjoyment of others.

8. Be Safe

Follow standard safety guidelines such as the following: Surf within your fitness level. Be sure you're strong enough to swim back to shore. Wear sunscreen. Stay within designated surf areas when riding patrolled beaches. Always surf with someone else.

9. Call for Help/Lend a Hand

If you need help, ask for it. Raise your hand in the air and call to others nearby. Surfers often find themselves in remote areas far from help. If you're out there, you're part of the community, so lend a helping hand.

10. Have Fun!

What's the point of surfing if you aren't having a good time? Relax, smile and enjoy your surfing and the others who are doing the same.

Jesse Hines:
East Coast Core

CHAPTER 17

It's a scene stuck on repeat around the world: teens, college students and adults drawn together, searching for something, seeking a way to escape pressures or boredom. They gather together in a club, on the beach, at a hotel or private home to pound drinks and hook up with some hot—or willing—girl or guy for a shot at some temporary pleasure.

The coastlines of the world play host to the scene on a regular basis. Maybe it's the Spring Break syndrome: travelers getting away and leaving their normal checks and balances at home. Maybe it's the boredom of a young generation looking for some fun, overloaded with the constant barrage of entertainment and electronic stimulation. Maybe it's the heightened longing, conscious or not, of something more that draws them to some of this world's most beautiful areas and then propels them toward shortsighted substitutes.

Jesse Hines knew the scene well. As a surfer growing up along the sleepy shores of Kitty Hawk, North Carolina, the teen lived for surf and the parties in between—until he and his whole crew

Vitals

Born: November 5, 1979

Home: Kill Devil Hills, North Carolina

Family: wife, Whitney

Sponsors: O'Neill, JC Hawaii, Adio, Spy, Speedfins, Outer Banks Boarding Company

Big Moment: *Noah's Arc* Tour

Favorite Break: Outer Banks

encountered God and found themselves swept into a drama much bigger than they could have imagined.

Nowadays, the freesurfer travels the world looking for dramatic waves to ride with his fluid style.

"He's a hot surfer, really stylish," *Surfing* magazine's associate editor Hagan Kelley says. "He's a full-on, Gerry Lopez-like style master—kind of from the old Hawaiian school, even though he's from the East Coast."

Yet even the thrill of exotic waves is less exciting to the goofy-footer than the changes he and his friends experienced as a result of their encounters with God.

PARTY MIX

To Jesse, the Outer Banks were a fickle tease, giving just enough hurricane-induced barrels to keep her admirers coming back for one more kiss, willing to endure her cold shoulder for the promise of what might be. Yet her summers were filled with indifferently flat seas as she spurned her followers, coyly shifting her sandbars to further an endless pursuit.

There was a lot of time to get in trouble, especially when small-town teenaged boredom was added to the mixture. "What do you want to do?" turned into new ways of getting into trouble, often fueled by the old standby: alcohol.

Virginia Beach, Virginia, a bigger city less than 100 miles up the coast, provided larger surf contests. Jesse and his friends headed there as much for the peripheral scene as for the regional competitions. Sure, they wanted to score good waves, but there were plenty of other extracurricular opportunities as well.

"Most surfers party because it's sort of the lifestyle," Jesse says. "There are hot girls in bikinis, and parties, and you have a lot of down time. For me at that age, partying was kind of the apex of it all."

On one particular weekend at Virginia Beach, Jesse and his friend Brandt Doyle surfed their heats and then found their own fun until the weekend was over. They met up again for the drive home, but something was different during the two-hour ride. Although the partying had been fun, the two groms were left feeling empty. "We started talking, and were like, 'Man, we've got to change. We've got to do something here,'" Jesse says.

That something was unclear at the time, but the conversation had stirred something deep inside the two teens.

"A couple months later we found out that the change we needed was to get back to God," Jesse says. "So we were like, 'Let's go to church.' It definitely was a turn of heart or a conscious move to get back to God."

Little did they know the end result would change their lives forever, transforming them on the deepest level and sweeping them into a movement that would reach beyond their greatest imaginations.

ROOTS MOVEMENT

Unknown to Jesse at the time, his friend and fellow surfer Noah Snyder was experiencing similar feelings and questions about his life. Noah's surfing had been going off and drawing major industry attention. The fellow Kitty Hawk local became the first Outer Banks surfer to go full-on pro.

Despite his success, the rising star was plagued by emptiness and questions about what his life meant. What was the point? Why did he feel so hollow when everything he'd always dreamed of was finally coming true? He was determined to find out, and church seemed like a good place to look for answers.

Jesse grew up attending church. As a 12-year-old, he asked Jesus to enter his life, but admittedly with little depth. "It was more like, 'Of course, I want to be a Christian. I want to go to heaven, so yeah, sure, I'll pray this prayer,'" he says. However, when Noah told the crew he was going to church, it all came together. Jesse and Brandt had also been feeling the pull toward God. All three, together with Jamie Smith, entered The Ark, a local church that was friendly to surfers.

"*Okay, God, I know I'm kind of messed up here, so I'm going to go to church. I'm going to try,*" Jesse says, describing his attitude. "*I don't really know how to do this, but I'm going to try to get back with You.*"

Jesse had made his move back toward God. Now it was God's turn to carry him the rest of the way.

The four friends were moved by the speaker at The Ark. When he invited listeners who wanted to surrender their lives to Jesus to raise a hand, Noah, Jamie and Brandt did. Then the speaker asked those who had responded to come forward.

"I don't think Noah was going to do it," Jesse says. "Then the friend who invited us saw Noah and said, 'I saw you raise your hand. You gotta come down there with me.' I was on the end, and when Noah and the other guys got up, I just followed them down there."

Although he had been moved by the speaker's message, Jesse hadn't felt an urgent need to raise his hand or walk forward. "It was almost like God picked me up and walked me down the aisle," he says. "It was cool, because I saw two friends from high school who were always faithful Christians. They came and prayed for me. It was a powerful, powerful moment. It was neat how God did it."

So what was the difference between Jesse's prayer as a 12-year-old and his experience at The Ark? "I came to an end [of myself], and I said, 'God, I need You. I don't really understand You, but I understand that I do need You,'" Jesse says. "God allowed me to make a bunch of bad decisions on my own and finally come to the point where I needed and wanted Him."

NEW SCHOOL

The crew had once been known for its stylish surfing and hard partying. After they became Christians, Jesse, Noah, Jamie and Brandt, along with brothers Brad and Matt Beacham, spent their time out of the water having Bible studies, learning about their new God, and experiencing a genuine depth in their relationships with each other. To this day, Jesse calls that group his best friends.

"Obviously, God had a plan," Jesse says. "He knew that we could support each other and ultimately grow to the place where we could do something like *Noah's Arc* and other things so that more people could be saved and added to the Kingdom."

Eight years after that Sunday at The Ark, Jesse and friends toured the East Coast, Europe and elsewhere around the world with the *Noah's*

Arc film. Jesse was always surprised when viewers told him he had done well in the movie. From his characteristically humble point of view, he had simply answered some questions and surfed. "It's really cool to see that you don't have to do anything except maintain a real relationship with God, just make yourself available, and He'll use you," Jesse says.

Jesse is a down-to-earth surfer with a slight North Carolina drawl. He has been able to travel the world getting mental in Indo, the Mentawais, Fiji, Hawaii and Australia, but his favorite spot is at home in the Outer Banks (when it's on, of course). He has modeled for Ralph Lauren, but he downplays that, too.

Competition is not Jesse's thing. He prefers his lower-key freesurfing set-up. Who wouldn't mind being paid by sponsors to travel the world in search of insane pits and left points (his favorite) to ride?

"Jesse is just as good as anybody in the world—just a brilliant surfer," says shaper John Carper, who sponsors Jesse. "We're always looking for the whole package [in our team riders]. We're looking for a guy who is a ripper, has good public persona—and a good-looking mug helps."

Jesse's take on the whole situation is characteristically mellow. "It's a blessing for me to be able to surf professionally," he says. "I just try to go find good waves."

Many of the thousands of people who attended *Noah's Arc* showings seemed to pick up the same vibe from Jesse and the others in the film. "The one thing that I always heard was the fact that it was so genuine, that people could feel God in it," Jesse says. "[People admired] the fact that it was so simple in that it was just what God was doing with us. There was nothing dressed up about it. I just kept hearing the word 'real.'"

Being real for Jesse begins with understanding and being thankful for God's love. "I just have to remember that God loves everybody, and so should I," Jesse says. "I'm no different than anyone, pro surfer or not. Whether it's Kelly Slater or some bum off the street, we're all created in the image of God, and He has a plan for us. I try to remember that I'm just part of the painting—one of the strokes of the brush."

Jesse tries to pass on that attitude to others. "Everyone is looking for something, and the one thing that is true is God," he says. "I always try to share that through my life and by my actions. I don't always do it, but that's what I want to do."

Being involved with *Noah's Arc* has been a highlight of Jesse's life. "That has definitely been the coolest experience for me as far as being a professional surfer and a Christian," he says. "I really felt like God was using me, and I wasn't really doing anything but making myself available to Him. Experiencing that with my friends has been a treasure that we'll always keep."

Passing Up Partying

Partying is fun at the time, and it seems like you're having a good time. But I know there are times when you get alone, and you're like, Man, this can't be all that life is. It's all kind of meaningless, like Solomon said in Ecclesiastes. He did it all, had all the money and the parties and the best wine and all the girls you could ever imagine, and he still said it was meaningless.

When you get in that place where you realize there has to be something that means something in this world, my advice is that the only thing that means anything is Jesus. You can try it all, but a relationship with Him is the one thing that will change your life forever. If you have the faith to say, "God, I desperately need You," He will change you.

—*Jesse Hines*

Spiritual Stoke

Surfing is spiritual for many, regardless of their belief in God (or lack thereof). Against a backdrop of faith, it is filled with metaphors of what it means to live in a moving, breathing flow with the Creator of the waves. Surfing is . . .

BEYOND WORDS

Ask a surfer to describe the feeling of surfing to someone who's never done it and you'll get answers similar to, "There's no way to describe it. It's beyond words." Those who attempt an explanation usually come back to the fact that it's something you've got to experience to understand. And there's no way to experience it but to dive in and ride the wave. You can watch from shore and maybe learn a lot, but you won't truly understand until you get your feet wet. Once you've experienced it, you share a bond with other surfers around the world.

Likewise, words can come up short when describing a relationship with Jesus. Yet all around the world, those who share a love for Christ share an eternal bond and oneness of purpose. All who seek after truth reach a point at which they have to take that final risk, that leap of faith, that complete surrender, and dive in.

BIGGER THAN YOU

Surfing is not about you. It's way bigger. The ocean's sheer volume is undeniable. Its power is humbling. You have to make the choice to paddle out. You have to build your skills and endurance. You even have to choose your wave. But in the end, the wave determines what kind of ride you will have.

God is all-powerful. The nature and the depth of His love leave little room for big egos. You have the choice to follow Him or not—daily. But you are barely the equivalent of a grain of sand to His ocean of power. Every step you take, every breath you breathe, is dependent on His mercy. Every life and every spiritual story is part of a vast and infinitely larger picture.

INVITING AND ADDICTING

One wave and you're hooked. The best ride of your life is exhilarating, but it urges you back to try to repeat its stoke. The surging ocean is always there. Its swells rise and fall, constantly changing, but always beckoning us to come and ride. When it's on, you're there. The addiction can be real, and some will abandon everything else in life to chase the ultimate wave.

God's love, grace and peace are life-changing. His call is constant, beckoning you always closer. His desire pulls you toward an ever-changing, ever-deepening relationship. When you get a taste, you want more. Somehow, spiritual sustenance from Jesus completely satisfies yet keeps you coming back for more.

A LIFESTYLE

Riding waves isn't a hobby; it's a lifestyle. Surfing becomes central to identity. You buy clothes by surf companies. You talk about waves and use wave-inspired lingo. You continue paddling out, improving your skills and becoming a more experienced waterman. You may order your time, career, or even your entire life around surfing.

The Ultimate Difference

No matter how amazing and fulfilling surfing can be, it is ultimately empty, temporary and fleeting. A string of flat days is enough of a reminder of that fact. Although life with Christ is overflowing, eternal and solid, the very thing that makes surfers spiritually sensitive is often the same thing that makes it difficult for them to surrender to God.

"The philosophy was a slogan for a surf company for many years: 'There is nothing that a good day of surfing won't cure,'" North Shore surfboard shaper John Carper says. "Surfing is a clean, wonderful, bright, beautiful, natural activity. A good day of surfing is really a wonderful thing. But because it depends on nature, it's only wonderful a few times a month. You go through dry spells, but then you get a nice day again when the sun's out and the water is blue and waves are good and the crowd's not bad, so you kind of get this redemption.

"Surfers are empty like everyone else, but there is always that feeling that the waves—and everything else—will be good again. They're always waiting for the new swell to come, the new surfboard, the new this and that. They are clean people, physically active and physically attractive. It's hard for people like that to be convicted."

Walking with Jesus isn't something you do; it's who you are. No matter what else a believer does in life, he or she is first and foremost a child of God. You can't put your identity in a box. It's not something reserved only for Sundays. God wants your undivided devotion. He longs for your best affection and desires to mark and shape your identity, your life and your soul with His absolute love.

PERSONAL

Remember your first wave? Remember the spot where the sun stood marking the time of day, the company watching and assisting you, the smell and taste of saltwater, the feeling of floating and flying when you stood up and were carried across the water's surface toward shore? Most surfers do. But ask 100 of them, and each story is different. There may be some similarities, but the specifics are unique for every individual. Even those too young to remember cherish an appreciation for that first wave.

Most Christians have a story of how they connected with Jesus and began their life with Him. As in the stories shared in this book, there are common threads of thoughts, emotions, fears, questions and encounters that run through many of them. But God is personal, drawing each individual to Himself in an intimate way. The details of each spiritual story are unique.

NOT A SPECTATOR SPORT

You meet someone on the beach, wearing the latest surf styles, carrying his board. He talks about surfing, knows stats on the pros, and tells you a great story about the time he almost died during an especially gnarly bail. But as you watch, you realize this guy never goes in the water. He's never paddled out or ever tried to catch a wave. Would you call him a surfer? No way. He's an imposter, a wannabe, a fake. You can't be a surfer from the shore. You've got to dive in.

Going to church, owning a Bible, knowing the right answers or wearing clothes from a Christian company means absolutely nothing on its own. You can't be a Christian until you give your life to Christ and continually dive into the depths of God's love and forgiveness.

ALL ABOUT THE STOKE

The guys and girls in this book are sick surfers. They have sponsors, win contests, travel the world, and get coverage in magazines, books and films. But when it comes down to it, the kid who grabs a few rides at sunrise before school or the girl who heads straight from work to her favorite break is just as much a surfer. The ability and visibility may be different, but the stoke is just as real.

There are "professional" Christians, too: pastors, missionaries, ministry leaders. But God is just as real to the guy who carves time out of his day to read the Bible. He is just as pleased with the girl who prays for her friend. And He is just as faithful to bless the $2 burrito you buy a homeless guy as He is to bless the millions of dollars dedicated to His work in faraway places.

First Waves

Matt Beacham

From the time I was 5 to the time I was 12, we lived right on the oceanfront in North Carolina. We lived in a part of town where it was all summer rental houses, so there was no one who lived within at least a mile of us. So we were out there alone, and my dad tried to push me into a wave. I was 7, and I went over the falls and wiped out. I turned around and told him, 'Dad, I'm never going to surf as long as I live; you'll see.' He started laughing at me. So about two years later, I finally stood up for like two seconds and jumped off screaming. My mom was on the beach. It was literally one of those things where I was like, "Did I just do that? That was insane. I can't believe it!"

Shannon McIntyre

When I was in second or third grade, my uncle would push me into waves on his longboard at Silver Strand Beach, where we'd go camping as a family. Several years later as a fifth grader, I caught my first stand-up wave by myself at Dog Beach in San Diego. My friend and I were side by side on our surfboards, and I stood up first because I had a big, junky, old single fin. She had a new thruster and never stood. The Lord gave me in that moment courage, faith and crazy joy. I felt like I was flying like an eagle. I felt like I was dropping in an elevator, even though it was probably a one-foot wave. I was so proud. I was in the fifth grade and hooked. I am so thankful to the Lord for the gift of surfing.

Kahana Kalama

I learned to swim when I was nine months old, even before I could walk. Growing up on the windward side of Oahu, I was always at the ocean, playing and bodyboarding. My dad is an outrigger canoe paddler, and all my family are watermen. I was raised to appreciate the ocean, whether it's surfing, canoeing, kayaking. I was seven years old when I first stood up on my own. My uncle pushed me into a wave on a 9-foot, 2-inch Ben Aipa longboard at Waikiki. I remember the crazy feeling of gliding along on the water's surface, and it hooked me for life.

Matt Beacham: Free Stylin'

CHAPTER 19

Ah, the life of a freesurfer. Wait and watch for remote storm surges to send pumping swells on to pristine breaks around the world. Could be Puerto Rico, the Maldives, maybe Panama or J-Bay. Then again, it could be exploring the sparse NorCal coast or Eastern Seaboard for tucked-away gems that are popping.

Wherever the destination, you've got to get yourself there to score some picture-perfect barrels or punt-worthy points—literally. Freesurfing is a job these days. The goal: deliver the shots and video clips that bring good exposure to your sponsors. No pressure to win (or even enter) contests. No chance at the big prize money of competition, either. But you're still getting paid to surf, enough to make a living. Is there a better job in the world?

It's a great era for living the surf life. Matt Beacham knows this well. "It's a total blessing that means I get to spend time enjoying God's creation," he says.

UNDER THE SURFACE

Home base is in the south O.C., but the goofyfooter's passport looks like some kind of international patchwork quilt: Australia, New Zealand, Peru, Costa Rica, Nicaragua, the Canary Islands,

Vitals

Born: October 30, 1977
Home: Alisa Viejo, California
Family: wife, Lily
Sponsors: Op, Cobian, Wave Riding Vehicles, Jet Pilot, X-Trak, Arnette
Big Moment: making the film *Foundnation* (1999)

Ireland, Bali, Sumatra, Puerto Rico, the Virgin Islands, Barbados, Mexico. And you don't even get passport stamps for crisscrossing the Hawaiian Islands and mainland United States.

All those prime spots have provided killer backdrops for Matt to showcase his aerial boosts and lip-bashing cutbacks in the service of his primary sponsor, Op. Although at 6 feet, 2 inches, he's big for a surfer, he's able to stay nimble and quick on waves.

"Matt is a dynamic surfer. He's got the X factor," says video lensman Nic McLean, who has spent many hours pointing a camera at Matt. "You never know what he's going to do. He has the ability to be very creative and spontaneous on the waves. He has a lot of aerial maneuvers. Half the time he's surfing backward."

"I never, ever thought I'd be able to pay some bills with surfing and travel and have a good time," Matt says. "Occasionally my wife can come with me, and we've seen quite a bit of the world together. And all the while God's doing this great thing of letting us do ministry the whole time."

Yeah, Beacham is stoked, for sure. The prospect of deserted curls can get him frothing, but if you really want to see him stoked, get him talking about Jesus. "Something beyond good waves or whatever—that's my main thing," Matt says. "I get pretty frustrated talking about nothing. The coolest thing to me is that with a Christian, you can cut right past the surf talk and launch right into something eternal."

TIGHT TIES

Maybe Matt's desire to cut past the chitchat and connect on a deeper level grows from the strong sense of community he developed as part of the well-documented Outer Banks crew that consisted of Noah Snyder, Jesse Hines and others.

Matt grew up on North Carolina's Outer Banks. From age 5 to 12, he lived in an oceanfront home in the town of Duck. It was there that he learned first to bodyboard, and then surf at age 7. Later, the family moved to Kitty Hawk.

The Outer Banks can be fickle, thanks to its ever-shifting sandbars, and wave hunting is as much a part of surfing as paddling out. "The day I got my license when I turned 16 was the biggest load off my shoulders ever," Matt says. "I could not believe that I actually got to drive myself to go surf. I couldn't get it through my head. I was like, *What? I actually get to drive myself? I won't have to beg my brother or parents to drop me off at the beach?*"

By the time he was 13, Matt's fluid skate-inspired riding style and East Coast contest wins had attracted attention. Wave Riding Vehicles added the grom to its team roster, and at 15, Matt was sponsored by Quiksilver.

The Beacham family was tight-knit. Mom and Dad were both Christians who provided a solid spiritual foundation for their boys,

Matt and Brad. "The way they handled us and faith was just epic," Matt says. "Nothing ever felt forced. It was just real."

Mom and Dad's example led to early belief in Jesus for Matt, but by late high school his faith had grown stale. It seems he had taken it for granted and become distracted by other more worldly pursuits. "I never derailed or anything, but enough to where I knew I was in rebellion," Matt says. "I knew I was turning my back on God in certain areas of my life."

When Matt attended college, he watched his older brother, Brad, apply a newfound seriousness to his spiritual life. It challenged and inspired Matt, who is one year younger.

Brad's influence spread, and when a friend joined Matt and his brother on a Hawaiian surf trip, the three began exploring the Bible together. "We were actually reading the New Testament the first time for ourselves, actually reading it straight through to figure out what's going on here," Matt says in *Noah's Arc*. "And we were having such a good time with it. God was doing so much repair in my heart."

During that trip, the boys' mom told them about the spiritual awakening taking place back home in the lives of their friends Noah Snyder, Jesse Hines, Brandt Doyle and Jamie Smith.

God was clearly up to something. The results would bring the crew closer than ever due to newfound spiritual connections. "Not only was God calling each person individually around me, He was letting us come together and enjoy the power of fellowship," Matt says. "God was so gracious to be working on us that way, loving us and showing us, *Hey, I've got plans for you, a better life. Seek Me in My Word.*"

And so they did. Matt began a Bible study in his apartment at the University of North Carolina, Wilmington. Every Monday night, 25 to 40 people would gather to pray, worship and look to the Bible for wisdom and guidance.

WORK AND PLAY

Spend any time around Matt and his friends and it's clear how much respect and appreciation others have for him. And how much they enjoy his company.

Good-natured, caring and funny, Matt is often looked to for comic relief—on camera or off. "I travel a lot with Will Tant and Matt Beacham, two of the funniest, coolest guys," says Matt Katsolis, film producer and head of Aquafluence Productions. "I love being around people who share the same love of laughter. I love hanging with them."

Film director Nic McLean goes back to college days with Matt. "He's genuine in his prayer and serious about doing right," Nic says. "He hates to see people done wrong. He's not the guy who plays pranks on everybody on trips. He's the guy who's always trying to be fair and nice. He's always been a ham. He knows that being a believer is fun and exciting, and he's just free."

Don't think Matt is only fun and games, though. *Surfing* magazine contributing photographer A.J. Neste admires his professionalism and calls him one of his favorite surfers to photograph. "I love the workhorse attitude of Beacham and Will Tant," A.J. says. "They work harder than anyone I know. It's fun to shoot with them, because I know they're not fooling around. They're not going out to do chop hop airs. They're going out there to get photos, to go big and go hard. They put so much feeling into their surfing."

MOVED BY MOVIES

Matt's route to a pro surfing career was different from most, thanks to the four years he spent at college.

"I was able to keep momentum through magazines and ads and stuff like that even while I was in college, which was bizarre," he says.

"It was the Lord's blessing. My sponsors knew it was enough momentum, and they saw the tiny window for me to pursue [a career] coming out of college. So they threw some peanuts at me to see what I could do."

Part of that momentum came through Matt's friendship with Nic McLean. The two met at Matt's college Bible study while Nic was completing his film school studies.

Matt had dreamed for years of making a surf movie with a spiritual message. "I used to turn the volume off on videos and watch the surf footage to my favorite Christian songs," Matt says. "It was full-on nerdy stuff, but God was doing something in my heart."

But with no movie-making experience, Matt wasn't able to get far in this dream. He saw a kindred spirit in Nic: someone who shared the passion and had the technical and artistic skills to pull it off. "Hey, man, what do you think about maybe doing a Christian surf movie?" Matt asked Nic one night after the Bible study.

Combined, the two created *Foundnation* in 1999 along the Outer Banks, and then followed with a sequel in 2000, *Foundnation Project*.

Like the West Coast boys of Walking on Water, the East Coast crew was cutting their early video teeth but beginning to make ripples of influence and personal impact. The films *The Outsiders* and *Noah's Arc* brought them all together. The progression has been amazing, as far as Matt is concerned.

"Some of the coolest guys I've ever met are the guys God has brought into the picture to work so hard for these ministry projects," Matt says. "They have a heart for the gospel and a heart for people, and all of a sudden I'm surrounded by these people. It's like I have to pinch myself. We get to do what we love and share it with people."

Knowing that God intersects lives through their efforts is Matt's greatest reward. He has toured with Walking on Water around the world for video outreaches in nations from Australia to Ireland to Peru. "To see people's lives changed through a video? It sounds bizarre, but it happens," he says. "The nights we do outreaches really are a turning point in a lot of people's lives."

Matt's enthusiasm can be contagious. His excitement for pointing others to God's wonders is encouraging, whether he's speaking to a crowd of Spanish speakers in Central America, inspiring a group of American youth pastors, or sending out hope to aspiring groms.

"No matter what age, you can literally seek God and make a decision to make your faith your own," he says, "to actually get real with yourself and realize what Jesus did on the cross and say, 'I'm going to do something about this right now. I'm going to come to God and believe in Him so strongly. I know He's going to be patient with me and train me in the way of the Word and give me peace about this crazy world that seems to always be seconds away from disaster.' To make that decision at a young age would be unbelievable."

Giving Back—Together

I can't believe I've gotten to see a lot of the world already with my wife, Lily. We went together to the Dominican Republic, where my wife used to go on missions trips. She'd been seven or eight times to build churches or help people rebuild houses, so she knew the place.

We got to go to Sri Lanka together for two full weeks of building with Habitat for Humanity. It was so neat to be able to do that and to work with Lily for a couple of weeks. She loves it. She loves getting out there and knowing that she's doing something. Then we were able to surf for a week at the end of the trip.

—*Matt Beacham*

The Search

CHAPTER 20

It may have been *Endless Summer* that popularized the quest for the perfect wave, but even before 1966, surfers were seeking the ideal curl. And that meant answering the call of remote coasts, islands, or anywhere else that might hold the Holy Grail of the oceans.

Surfers have always been mobile. Perhaps it's the inherent nature of a sport based on motion or the necessity of one played out on a constantly shifting field. At any rate, even ancient Hawaiian royalty often transported their boards with them during inter-island journeys. In the early twentieth century, Hawaiian surfers Duke Kahanamoku and George Freeth became itinerant ambassadors, bringing surfing to the world. By the 1920s, modern wave-riding pioneers such as Tom Blake were finding their way to Hawaii to explore the islands' waves of wonder. And by the '50s, movies and magazines began to regularly focus on the exploration for surf, whether it meant a day's jaunt from home or an intercontinental voyage.

"Surfers are the best-traveled sportsmen in the world," pro-surfer turned journalist Dave Parmenter says in *The Encyclopedia of Surfing.* "We've become the widest-flung tribe of fanatics since the Jesuits."[1]

Like the rest of the sport, surf travel has evolved. The 1980s opened the doors to commercial surf tourism after the first pay-to-stay establishment, Grajagan Surf Camp, opened in 1978 in Java. It offered fairly sparse accommodations and immediate access to G-Land's beautiful breaks. The Tavarua Island Resort upped the

Surfing the Nations: Ready to Go

This generation of surfers will go! That's the message of Surfing the Nations, a Honolulu, Hawaii, based ministry run by Tom and Cindy Bauer, Youth With a Mission-trained missionaries. Surfing the Nations reaches out in the name of Jesus through international surf missions, and targets especially the countries of the 10/40 Window (the zone of largely Muslim nations between the tenth and fortieth parallels). Surfing the Nations believes that by providing disaster relief and medical assistance and by meeting the tangible needs of the poor around the world, surf missions will change world missions.

"Surfers are mission-ready," says Tom. "We have dreamed about going to nations. We love adventure. We'll eat anything. We'll sleep anywhere. We are ready to go."

The global explosion in interest and fascination with surfing has opened doors to surfers that would otherwise be closed. "The mandate of Surfing the Nations is lifestyle evangelism," Cindy says. "So you surf. Surfing is tailor-made for missions, because they expect you to hang out with the local people. They expect you to sit around with your guitar and play music. You just sing praises and worship God the whole time."

Surfing the Nations believes God is calling surfers to get involved in His bigger picture around the globe. "The gospel message never changes," Tom says. "But the way we communicate it does. Surfing is a powerful way to share the gospel and glorify God."

There are definite challenges to this type of ministry, but it's a dream come true for Tom and Cindy. "I always dreamed about going on the endless summer," Tom says. "When I said yes to God as a surfer, I'm finding I'm actually [living the endless summer]. God is a God of adventure, and He loves the nations of the world."

The Bauers view surfing as much a calling as a fun sport. "God has called us as surfers to impact the nations," Tom says. "And I believe our surfboards are our pulpits."

ante in the early '80s. Often called the Club Med of surfing, the resort provides plush accommodations and access to the "perfect wave"—Cloudbreak.

The 1990s and 2000s placed mobility back at the forefront as tour operators in Indonesia began transporting paying clients between firing reef breaks via chartered boats. And now wave seekers don't even have to set foot on shore: the *Indies Trader IV* provides charter trips with luxurious on-board accommodations and toys including jet skis and a helicopter used for aerial surf reconnaissance.

Despite the more glamorous recent offerings, the heart of surf travel will always retain its free-flowing simplicity. Go light, roll with the conditions, hitch rides. Sleep on the beach, in the car, on a friend's floor or in an inexpensive hostel. Eat cheap, scrounge, or starve. It's all about the waves and the experience of far-flung cultures. There's a beautiful unencumbered freedom in the process.

Yet all is not ideal. Unfortunately, some wave riders have given surfers a bad reputation around the world with their me-first mentality and greed-driven sense of entitlement. For those individuals, the process is all about taking—taking waves, taking resources, taking girls, taking pleasure, and then taking off. Have we become modern-day pirates and conquistadors? Is it any wonder when localism and resentment arise in Third World lineups and beach towns?

Thankfully, surfers are discovering another way. A collective conscience is rising. There are those who are looking beyond themselves, seeking to listen and learn from the cultures they visit. They are realizing the blessings they've been given materially as First World citizens and emotionally as surfers and acting from a sense of thankfulness and responsibility.

Those answering to the tenets of this new global tribe are not limited by spiritual boundaries, but many of its members are marked by their belief in Jesus. They are those who take seriously Christ's command to love our neighbor—next door or a world away—as much as we do ourselves. They are those who understand that humanity's greatest need is spiritual, but who also realize that God values our physical condition as well. They listen to the Bible's directives to feed the hungry and clothe the naked.

These surfers will go in search of waves with open hearts and open hands. They will share the bounty of waves and offer what they can humanly, physically and spiritually to those they encounter. They will make a difference, perhaps small at first, but growing. And in return for giving, they will discover that they have received more than the waves can offer, and more than they could have imagined.

"I've been on surf trips where it's all about surfing only, and I've been on surf trips where we do outreaches and visit orphanages and give back," says Mike Doyle, director of outreach for Walking on Water. "The ones when we gave back were literally a hundred times better than when we just went and surfed. Surfing is empty, ultimately. But when you use surfing to serve God and reach people with the gospel, it's the most insane life there is."

Open your eyes. Open your heart. Open your hands. Join the movement.

Send Hope: Next Door and Abroad

Tom and Cindy Bauer's heart for the people of the world starts right at home, on the island of Oahu, Hawaii. Through Send Hope, a division of Surfing the Nations, they bring hope to the hopeless by providing a launch pad for volunteer-based assistance to the hurting and deprived. Two of their ministries, Feeding the Hungry and Youth-At-Risk, provide help for the often unseen, hurting people of Hawaii.

"Because Hawaii is beautiful, it covers up a lot of sin," says Cindy. "Our place is actually stationed between two known drug houses. So we started out feeding 7 different families through just a simple delivery from the back of my car, and now we're feeding 1,500 people. It's one of the largest food drops and food centers for feeding the hungry of Hawaii.

"We reach out to the homeless as well as to the financially struggling. The people will say, 'This is the only place where I feel like people care.' Because we've loved them, they're very loving to us. For some of them, it's the only bit of gospel that they see. During the day that we feed the hungry, we also run a full-on Bible study and a class teaching English as a second language.

"Our Youth-At-Risk program is multifaceted. It includes a weekly Bible study in hopes of providing our next generation with a safe, fun place to hang out where they will hear a positive message. We are also involved in the surf club at a local high school.

"We believe that God is beginning to do a massive move within the Body of Christ to say, 'We need to take care of the poor again.' We've pretty much dumped it all on government and said, 'You do it. We don't have to worry about it.' And we've lost the poor, and we've lost the schools.

"The world is hurting. Together, we are sending hope."

Endnotes

Chapter 1—C.J. Hobgood: World Champion

1. Matt Walker, "Dude Be Not Proud," *Surfing* magazine, March 2002.
2. C.J. Hobgood, quoted in *The Surfers Bible*, Christian Surfers International, 2002. http://www.christiansurfers.net/surfersbible_personal.htm (accessed May 2006).
3. Justin Cote', "Hobgoods²: C.J. and Damien Hobgood Decide They Can't Fight Nature," *Transworld Surf*, July 2005.
4. "Pro Spotlight," *Transworld*.

Chapter 2—Out of the Deep

1. Peter Benchley and Judith Gradwohl, "'Ocean Planet' Oceanographic Facts" and *Ocean Planet: Writings and Images of the Sea* (New York: Harry N. Abrams Inc., 1995), n.p.

Chapter 5—Tom Curren: Icon on a Search

1. Matt Walker, "400ᵗʰ Issue: Generation Now—Interview with Tom Carroll," *Surfing*, June 2005.
2. Chris Mauro, "Interview: Occy on Being a Rock Star, Fatherhood, Curren, Irons, Slater, and a Whole Lot More," *Surfer*, December 2004.
3. Matt Warshaw, "Curren, Tom," *The Encyclopedia of Surfing* (Orlando, FL: Harcourt, Inc., 2003), p. 145.
4. Drew Kampion, *The Way of the Surfer* (New York: Harry N. Abrams, Inc., 2003), p. 136.
5. Ibid.
6. Chris Mauro, "The Surfer Interview: Tom Curren," *Surfer*, April 2004.

Chapter 6—Taking Shape: A Brief History of the Board

1. Nic McLean and Bryan Jennings, Introduction to *Noah's Arc* video, Walking on Water, 2004.

Chapter 7—Al Merrick: The Shape of Legends

1. Evan Slater, "Al Merrick: Surfing's 2004 Shaper of the Year," *Surfing*, February 2005, p. 80.
2. Ibid.

Chapter 8—Once You're In, You're In

1. Dana Brown, "Serious Fun, No Matter What," in *Step Into Liquid* (Houston, TX: Top Secret Productions, 2003).

2. William Finnegan, *The Encyclopedia of Surfing* (Orlando, FL: Harcourt, Inc., 2003), p. viii.
3. Sanoe Lake, "Ten Ways to Impress Sanoe Lake," *Transworld Surf,* November 2005.
4. Shannon McIntyre, "Faith," *Shannon Surf.* http://www.shannonsurf.com (accessed May 2006).

Chapter 9—Bethany Hamilton: Surfing's Survivor

1. Bethany Hamilton with Sheryl Berk and Rick Bundschuh, *Soul Surfer* (New York: Pocket Books/MTV Books, 2004), p. 70.
2. Ibid., pp. 159-160.
3. Pat Milton, "Teen Surfing Champ Inspires Tsunami Orphans," Associated Press, *Honolulu Star-Bulletin,* September 22, 2005.
4. Alexandre Da Silva, "Bethany Rides Again," Associated Press, *Honolulu Star-Bulletin,* November 19, 2005.
5. Evan Slater, "'05 O'Neill Women's Challenge at Sunset Beach: Melanie Redman-Carr Wins Women's Surfing Event," *Surfing,* December 1, 2005.
6. Da Silva, "Bethany Rides Again."

Chapter 12—Deeper Than Appearances

1. Brad Melekian, "USD Professor's Course Opens New Door into Surf Culture, History, Surfing," *San Diego Union-Tribune,* February 28, 2006.
2. Conor Dougherty, "Soles and Inspiration," *San Diego Union-Tribune,* December 7, 2003, p. N4.

Chapter 13—Aaron Chang: Capturing Living Light

1. Matt Warshaw, "Chang, Aaron," *The Encyclopedia of Surfing* (Orlando, FL: Harcourt, Inc., 2003), p. 116.
2. Ibid.

Chapter 14—The Motion of Pictures

1. Matt Warshaw, *Surf Movie Tonite! Surf Movie Poster Art 1957-2005* (San Francisco, CA: Chronicle Books, 2005), n.p.

Chapter 16—Whose Wave Is It?

1. "Keeping the Pact," *Risen,* vol. 4, no. 2, 2005.

Chapter 20—The Search

1. Matt Warshaw, "Surf Travel," *The Encyclopedia of Surfing* (Orlando, FL: Harcourt Inc., 2003), p. 591.